STRESS-FREE
RETIREMENT

STRESS-FREE
RETIREMENT

STRESS-FREE
RETIREMENT

Patrick Kelly

Stress-Free Retirement

Cover and Interior Design by The Impact Partnership

ISBN 978-0-9833615-2-7

Printed in the USA

"It wasn't raining when Noah built the ark."

Howard Ruff

"The quickest way to double your money is to fold it over and put it back in your pocket."

Will Rogers

To SAA - Thank you for making this possible

TABLE OF CONTENTS

Acknowledgements

A completed book is a symphony, not a solo. No author is a one-man band. And in this orchestra I have many I'd like to thank.

First and foremost to my wife, Marly, for not only being the best first-draft editor I know, but also for the many single-parent evenings a book project entails.

To Art Moore, a final editor par excellence.

To Christophe Laurenceau and Chris Sandlin, the best design folks in the business. You took my words and made them art. They say you can't judge a book by its cover; but in this case, I sincerely hope people do.

To all the insurance representatives around the country who allowed me to interview them for the pages that follow. *You* are the real heroes of this book. The ones who carry the melody line. Thank you for your tireless efforts as you seek to help individuals protect and grow what they've accumulated. This book would not exist without you.

And lastly, to all those not individually named, who gave their time to read drafts, provide thoughts, and make this a better book. Please know that what you offered blends with the rest of the orchestra to create a harmony that would not have been possible without your contribution.

Patrick Kelly, February 2013

Important Disclosure

Please Read

Ahhhh ... don't you just love disclosures? Like those pharmaceutical commercials on television that conclude with the fast talking man who describes all the ills a particular medicine may inflict – heart attack, stroke, paralysis, and ... death. Wait a minute! Wasn't I just trying to lower my blood pressure? But I'm certain you understand *why* those disclosures exist. They are a significant and important aspect of consumer protection, not only in the pharmaceutical world, but in the financial world as well. So with that said, I have a few important disclosures and clarifications I'd like to make *before* you begin this book.

First, I hope you understand that a title is simply that – a title. It promises nothing more than a catchy phrase in hopes of getting a book picked off the shelf. And so it is with *Stress-Free Retirement*. Please know this is simply a title – not a promise. I can't guarantee you a "stress-free" retirement any more than I can fly you to the moon. No one can.

Also, please know that I salt my chapters with humor. Lots of different forms of humor, including some occasional sarcasm.

Next, *I want to state unequivocally that this book is not intended to give any investment, legal, or tax advice of any kind*. Not an ounce. As a matter of fact, this book promises nothing more than a couple hours of reading. Hopefully *enjoyable* reading. However, if you don't like it, just consider it an inexpensive sleep aid with fewer side effects than prescription meds.

And lastly, I need to get a little technical and state some specific and important disclosure information.

• For the purpose of readability I may refer to financial professionals in many different manners – advisor, representative, agent, broker, etc. – please know this is not intended to be an indication or a reference as to what an individual may or may not be duly licensed to sell; rather, it is colloquial terminology in order to avoid mind-numbing monotony. It is your job as a consumer to make sure that the individual you choose to work with is properly licensed to sell the product you desire to purchase.

• Throughout this book I may also use many different terms for accumulation of money – "returns," "gains," "upside potential," "growth," "share of market gains," and likely others. Please know that this is also simply colloquial phrasing and that any reference to the growth within a Fixed Indexed Annuity is intended to mean "interest credited," since that is the only way in which a Fixed Indexed Annuity grows in value.

• It is important to understand that a Fixed Indexed Annuity is not a securities product.

• Please know that this book is not intended to make any comparison between different types of products, Fixed Indexed Annuities, or others. Also, it is not the scope or intention of this book to give all the necessary details needed in order to purchase any specific product. The purchase of any product should only be considered after a face-to-face meeting with a properly licensed and knowledgeable representative, as is encouraged many times throughout this book. Also, I am a big believer that an individual should do his or her own homework as well. Run the numbers. Ask the questions. Do the math. Read the product literature. Only then will he or she know if a product provides the proper fit for his or her specific needs. Also, keep in mind that any fair and actual comparison between one product and another, of any kind, should have all material differences identified, including differences in investment objectives, sales and management fees, liquidity, risks, guarantees, insurance aspects, fluctuation of principal and/or return, tax treatment, as well as a multitude of other items, none of which this book is intended to do.

• Let me be clear on something. *Nothing* is risk free. And while I don't believe I ever make such a statement in this book, I want to be incredibly forthright about that statement. Everything has risk of some kind. Market risk. Inflation risk. Opportunity cost risk. And many other possible types of risks. While Fixed Indexed Annuities minimize risk in many important areas, they do not eliminate risk altogether. Also, any guarantees provided by annuities are subject to the claims paying ability of the issuing company, which is a risk in itself.

• Fixed Indexed Annuities, like any financial product, need a full and detailed explanation of their many unique features. In particular, with Fixed Indexed Annuities, the consumer should seek full understanding of such things as "caps," "fees," "spreads," "participation rates," "crediting methodologies," "bonuses," "bonus recapture," and any other feature that a particular product may provide. Again, it is not the intention or scope of this book to detail those items; that should be discussed in a face-to-face meeting with a licensed and knowledgeable representative in your local area.

• Please know that the terms "safe" and "secure," when used to describe an insurance product, including a Fixed Indexed Annuity, are references to, and based solely upon, the financial strength and claims paying ability of the issuing company.

It is my hope that this book will simply be a *starting point* in your financial journey. Not an ending point. Please do not make any financial or purchasing decisions … of any kind … based on the words in this book. That should be done only after a thorough and proper conversation with a properly licensed professional. Please know I wish you nothing but the very best, both now and in the years to come. Happy reading.

Preface

My first two books, *Tax-Free Retirement* and *The Retirement Miracle,* are only half of the story. There's more. Much more. And I have been dreaming about this book for six years. It's the story that needs to be told for the *other* half of the population – those individuals already *in,* or near, retirement. Those individuals desperate to protect the retirement nest egg they've worked so hard to accumulate. Those individuals wanting to exit the roller coaster of terrifying market swings and live a peaceful and rich retirement, both financially and emotionally.

But please know that nothing in this book negates the paramount message from my first two. Those principles are as significant today as ever. Maybe even more so. Rather, this book is like the final stage of a long journey. A journey that each potential retiree will make as he or she ponders the transition from workplace to retirement, and all the implications that come with that change.

So, while my first two books are aimed primarily at those

who are *still in their saving years*, this book is designed for those individuals *who have already accumulated a nest egg they'd like to protect*, for those who desire to live their retirement years in peace – without spending their days fretting over the ravages of market volatility or inflation.

If that sounds compelling, then this book is for you. And it's my desire that it will add both money and quality of life to your golden years.

And let me clearly state one other thing. This book is *not* intended to give tax or legal or investment advice of any kind. For those types of questions I encourage you to seek the counsel of a capable and properly licensed professional. The purpose of this book is simply to open your eyes to some powerful concepts and opportunities that could possibly enhance your financial peace of mind – and to provide a little fun along the way.

However, the only way to know if these strategies will meet your personal needs is to meet with a local and licensed representative who can evaluate your particular situation. A representative who can delineate the advantages and disadvantages of all your options and help you sort out what is best suited to your unique position. The principles and concepts in this book are *not* a "one-size-fits-all" solution. Nothing is. However, as always, I encourage you to check it out, look at the facts, and decide for yourself.

I wish you all the best on this final stage of your financial journey.

PART 1: THE DILEMMA

Chapter 1

The Poker-Chip Mentality

The first time I ever set foot into a casino was in the Bahamas. I was 18 years old and on a post-high-school-graduation trip that was given to me as a gift. I was in awe.

Since I'd never been in a casino before, I remember being completely enamored as I watched all of the sunburned tourists throw their money away on the green felt. I stood. I wandered. I didn't want to leave.

As I made my way through the smoke-filled room, my eye was drawn to a young man, likely in his early 30s, playing Blackjack one-on-one with a dealer. He was sitting next to an attractive blonde sporting diamonds the size of golf balls. Now Blackjack was a game I did happen to know. So I stopped. What caught my eye next was the unique color of chips that towered in front of the man. Chips a color I hadn't seen sitting in front of any other player. I was curious, so I stepped closer and thought my eyes were playing a trick on me.

These were not $25 chips or $100 chips – they were $1,000 chips! Seriously!? $1,000 chips!? I did some quick counting and figured this guy had about $50,000 worth of chips sitting in front of him. Fifty-thousand dollars! I was hooked.

As I watched intently, a few things became quickly apparent. One, this guy knew his stuff at a Blackjack table. Two, he devoured the attention from the growing crowd. And three, this was all about trying to impress the gal sitting next to him.

So let me tell you what happened next.

In the course of five short minutes, not a minute more, this young man built his chip stack from $50,000 to over $150,000. I was in shock. I couldn't believe it. *A hundred-thousand-dollar gain! In five minutes!*

I wanted him to stand up. Walk away. Cash it in. Call it good. Collect his winnings and go buy himself a bright red Ferrari. But needless to say, he *didn't* stand up. He *didn't* cash it in. He *didn't* walk away. And what he did next left me completely flabbergasted.

You know what's coming, don't you?

He started losing. And losing big. While in the previous five minutes he couldn't *lose* a hand, now he couldn't *win* one. And his bets became bigger and bigger and BIGGER. And in the next three minutes he … lost … it … all.

Wow! One hundred and fifty thousand dollars blown in three minutes. Crazy. My 18-year-old brain couldn't comprehend such a thing was even possible. It seemed to me, at the time, that such activity should be illegal. Outlawed. (I guess that's why it *is* illegal in most parts of the world.)

I saw at that moment that casinos have a trick. That the game is rigged. Not just statistically rigged, but emotionally rigged as well. That's their *real* advantage. You see, a casino plays by odds – cold, hard, emotionless rules. Rules that stack the game in their favor. The gambler, however, plays by emotion – greedy, optimistic emotion. And in the long run, odds eat emotion for lunch – every time.

Let me ask you a question. Why do you think casinos invented poker chips? Was it because real money got lost on the green felt? Of course not. It's because poker chips aren't real currency. They don't pay the mortgage or the light bill. They don't put food on the table or tackle the kids' tuition. And if they're not real, then it doesn't feel like losing real money. That's their secret. If you keep a measured distance between people and their money, you can quietly take it away from them – all of it.

Here's what I wonder. What if there *had* been an actual Ferrari or a three-bedroom house sitting in front of that young man instead of just a pile of chips? Would he have wagered them on the turn of a few random cards? Maybe, but not very likely. Why? Because a car is real. A house is real. You can touch it, see it, and smell it.

The casino knows that if it can distance a player from his money, he is likely to gamble more, risk more, and lose more, because he perceives he is not losing real money but just some cheap, plastic chips.

But here's the frustrating part of all this. Casinos are not the only ones playing this game. As a matter of fact, they're not even the biggest culprits. There is an establishment much more dangerous. It's called Wall Street. Wall Street is playing the same game as the casino, but on a much larger scale. Let me explain what I mean when I say it is more dangerous. One difference between a casino and Wall Street is that a casino is required by law (at least in the state of Nevada) to give you the exact odds of every game in its establishment. Wall Street is not.

Did you know that about casinos? Most people don't. Try this.

Walk up to a cashier in a Nevada casino and ask him for an "odds sheet." He's required to give you one. At least it's a losing game *with full disclosure.*

Now, try asking Wall Street that same question. Ask them for an "odds sheet" on your investment portfolio. Yeah … good luck. There is absolutely no such thing. Why? *Because no one knows the odds of the market.* No one! Wall Street doesn't know. Their analysts don't know. No one knows. It's simply a gamble. A roll of the dice. A bet. And sometimes you win. And sometimes you lose.

The problem with Wall Street, just like the Blackjack table, is that investors are spurred on by the same three characteristics as the gambler – emotion, greed, and optimism – which usually combine to make for really poor financial decisions.

And just like the young man who lost all his chips in a few short minutes, over the years, many "investors" have found their brokerage accounts wiped out by margin calls and market losses, simply because they were betting bigger and bigger on a position they were certain couldn't lose.

The only problem is, it can lose and it *does* lose. And only when the pain becomes severe enough, and optimism turns to abject terror, does the stock investor sell everything and flee the market, although usually only *after* crippling losses. I saw this very thing happen in 2001 with the bursting of the tech bubble, as told in chapter one of my first book, *Tax-Free Retirement.* (Unfortunately, I actually *participated* in 2001. That's why I know these feelings and this cycle so well.) And then I watched the very same thing unfold again, seven short years later, during the credit crisis of 2008, but this time with greater panic and steeper losses.

But the similarity between the casino and Wall Street goes even deeper. Wall Street has learned the significance of the poker-chip mentality. They've developed their own variation called a *"paper"* loss. Rarely, if ever, do you hear them call it what it really is. A loss. Plain and simple. They mask it like a little plastic chip. Think about it. When was the last time you heard someone say, "I'm sorry Mr. Smith, this month you lost the equivalent of a four-bedroom house in your portfolio."

What!? They didn't tell you that!?

Of course they didn't; because as soon as a "paper" loss became a tangible, real, or measureable loss, people would flee the market like rats off the proverbial sinking ship. As a matter of fact, Wall Street even has the audacity to verbalize this very thing by saying, "Don't worry about it Mr. Smith. You don't have a *'real'* loss. It's just a paper loss. You won't experience an actual loss unless you sell your position."

C'mon. Really? The last time I checked, a "paper" loss *was* a "real" loss. A real loss that just hasn't been experienced yet. And why do they call it this? Because as long as it's just a "paper loss," it's just a poker chip. Distant. Plastic. Artificial.

But these paper losses have brought down more economies, put more people out of business, and put more retirements on hold than all the casinos in the world could ever imagine. They're lethal, and they're real.

But there *is* an answer to this madness. As a matter of fact, this book was written for that very purpose – to show you that there *is* a way to stack the odds in your favor and to never take a market loss again.

Think about that. Imagine a Blackjack table where the worst you could do was "push" with the dealer. Break even. Better yet, what if there was a way to keep a percentage of every winning hand yet never give back a penny on your losing hands? How popular would *that* table be? It would have a line of players that stretched from Vegas to the Pacific Ocean. The only problem is that the line would never get shorter because those sitting at the table would never leave. Why would they? Because people sitting at that table would no longer be "gambling" – they would simply be "winning." They would either be making a little money or breaking even on every hand.

Think about that. How would you like to play a game that guaranteed you'd make money on every winning hand and break even on every losing hand? Now that's a game I want to play.

Well … here's the good news. You *can*. But it's not a game. You *can* participate in a strategy that will offer you growth in the winning years while guaranteeing your account will *never* take a market loss in the bad years. I know that seems too good to be true. But, fortunately, it's not. It's real. It's possible. And I'm going to explain to you exactly how this strategy works, and more importantly, how you can set yourself up to participate.

However, before we get to the details of exactly how you can accomplish this, I'd like to share a few stories. So sit back. Relax. Pour yourself a nice cup of coffee – and enjoy.

Chapter 2

A Ho-Hum 17 Percent*

I'd like for you to meet a woman named Judy. Why Judy? Simple. Because Judy perfectly embodies the current thought process of today's retirement clientele. A thought process that many financial professionals fail to understand.

But even more importantly, I want you to know that Judy is not some fictitious character of my imagination. She is a real person and this is her real story, as it was related to me by one of America's top financial professionals. An individual I'll hypothetically call David for the sake of this story.

Judy was a 70-year-old stock market veteran who had zero interest in changing her current course of action. She was happy and content with her stock portfolio, especially since it had recovered so well in the five years since the tech crash of 2000-2001. However, even with all of her stubborn resistance to change, one of Judy's closest friends insisted she meet with David, who specialized in protecting clients' money from loss. And so she reluctantly agreed.

David remembers the day well. It was a beautiful, sunny day late in the summer of 2006, and into his office walked a redheaded, bright-eyed, firecracker of a woman. Not an inch over five feet tall. She was all business. Judy kept the introduction short and jumped right in, not wasting a second before she began putting David through his paces.

Judy explained to him that she was a veteran of the stock market and had ridden the ups and downs of many market cycles through the decades. She also explained that she had fared pretty well and therefore wasn't looking to do anything differently. She was only there at the prompting of a good friend.

David didn't flinch. He loved these situations and found them to be some of the most enjoyable throughout his year. He began asking Judy some important questions and soon found out that she was tired of watching the daily fluctuations of the stock market. She expressed a desire to put her money on autopilot and live her days untethered from the financial television networks. She found it draining and knew it was keeping her from other, more significant activities.

David understood her thinking and was excited to show her a new strategy. A strategy that would not only protect her money from loss but also free her time for more important activities like enjoying her grandchildren and traveling the world.

Judy was impressed.

David and Judy got back together about a week later, and Judy decided to throw him a bone. She told him she was going to let him assist her with $300,000 of her IRA money.

And just as David does with every client, he went to work and found what he believed to be the right product for Judy. A product with zero stock market risk. Zero stock market volatility. And the potential for very solid returns.

Judy became a client.

Now fast-forward 12 months to the summer of 2007. Judy returned to David's office for her first annual review. David was excited for the meeting and as proud as a peacock in full array. He'd dusted his office, organized his chairs, and could hardly wait to give Judy the incredible news: The $300,000 she had given him 12 months previous had grown by a whopping 17 percent – in an interest-rate-based product that presented zero stock market risk. He could hardly wait. These were the appointments he lived for.

As Judy took a seat at the conference table, David wasted no time. "Judy, I am so excited to see you!" he said. "What a great year we've had! Your account went up 17 percent."

"Yeah, I saw that on the statement. That's good," Judy said with little expression and less enthusiasm.

He was dumbfounded. He couldn't believe her reaction. She must have misunderstood something. So again he said, "No, wait Judy, not *7* percent but *17* percent! *Seventeen!* Can you believe that?"

Still, Judy gave him nothing. Not even a glimmer. She said, "Yeah, I know. That's fine. The stock market did 24 percent, and I did 17. I guess that's good."

"But Judy, you have to realize that this *isn't* the stock market. This is a *fixed product*. And you earned *17 percent* in a fixed vehicle. This is a safe and conservative strategy, and you did *17 percent!*"

But even with all of David's excitement, she just wouldn't budge.

She said, "I hate to break this to you, but at my age you're just not going to get me to do any cartwheels. Sorry. It's just not going to happen."

He was totally befuddled.

David's excitement stemmed from the obvious fact that any double-digit return in a fixed product is something to crow about. That's not the norm. Although he'd seen some of his clients experience a few unusually good years in the 20-plus percent range, he'd never seen anybody – *ever* – cast aside a 17-percent return as just a ho-hum event.

He and Judy continued their conversation, and at the end of the meeting, as they parted ways, he said, "I do hope you're happy about this year's performance. And while I'm sure I'll see you sometime in the next few months, if I don't, I look forward to seeing you back here in 12 months for your next annual review."

And so they parted.

He did see Judy a couple of times throughout that year at different client appreciation events he hosted in his community. They said hello and chatted briefly. But it wasn't until the next annual review that they took the opportunity to visit at length.

And this second review happened to fall right at the end of 2008, just as the markets were in the middle of their death spiral due to the collapse of Lehman Brothers and the vast and unexpected credit freeze. The markets were cratering; and because of that, Judy's account had a *zero-percent return* in her second year.

He was *not* looking forward to *this* appointment. He was preparing for the worst. If 17 percent didn't cause Judy to crack a smile, what was *zero percent* going to do for her? He was sweating bullets.

D-Day arrived, and in walked Judy. David was sure his eyes were playing tricks on him. What was in her hands? Was it a plate of brownies? Indeed it was. And not only was she carrying a gigantic plate of brownies, but she marched right up to David's six-foot-three frame, wrapped her slender arms around his waist, and gave him a great big hug. As she let go, she looked up into his face, and he could see there were tears in her eyes.

"You really have no idea how grateful I am to have known you over this last year," she said.

"Wait a second Judy. Hold on. Whoa! Last year you got a 17-percent return and didn't give me as much as a twinge of a smile – nothing – and now this year when you get a big, fat zero, you walk in with a plate of brownies and a hug!?"

"Yes. That's right. You see, I've been talking to my friends. Talking to my neighbors. Talking to my family. All of them have lost money in the last few months. Some of them *a lot* of money. But I haven't lost a dime. And not only that, but I *still* see last year's 17-percent return in my account. One of the smartest things I *ever* did in my entire life was to listen to my friend who told me to come and see you. By the way, *she* got a plate of brownies, too!"

David smiled. "Thank you, Judy. I appreciate that."

"This is the best zero I ever received," Judy said.

And indeed it was.

Folks, *this* is the all-important mentality that so many financial professionals completely miss. While growth is important, protecting your client's hard-earned money against loss is even more important. Eliminating losses becomes critical at a certain point in an individual's life, because eliminating losses eliminates pain and uncertainty. Two things most retirees would prefer to do without.

And why do I share with you Judy's story? I do so hoping it will excite you to learn about a strategy that will eliminate losses but not eliminate growth; a strategy that will have you baking brownies and giving hugs when you see a big, fat, zero-percent return on your account statement, because you'll know that a zero for you means most other people *lost* money. But not you. And not David's dear friend, Judy.

* The results and performance Judy received in this story occurred in the past. It should not be inferred that any such results can or will be achievable either now or in the future.

Chapter 3

Mr. Bankman

When not losing money becomes a primary objective, most individuals turn to their local bank. I'd like to explain why that may not be the best idea. To do so, I'd like for you to meet another person. A person we all know and a person we all trust. But a person who might not be exactly what he seems. His name? Mr. Bankman. And just like the Wizard hiding behind the curtain in the city of Oz, I'd like to give you a glimpse behind the curtain of Mr. Bankman's life. (But first I must point out, so you don't think I'm assailing all those wonderful people working at your local banking institution, that Mr. Bankman is **not** an individual; rather, he's an *institution*, an institution that may not always put *your* best interest at the top of its priority list.)

So, let's meet this allegorical Mr. Bankman.

Mr. Bankman wakes up each morning and puts on a blue, pinstriped suit, a freshly starched white shirt, and his best red tie. Mr. Bankman has never bought into casual Fridays, because he has an image to uphold. His shoes are polished, and his car is waxed. You see, Mr. Bankman wants you to believe he's as patriotic as baseball and apple pie. And he works hard – very hard – to gain your trust so that you'll always look to him as the pinnacle of financial safety within your community.

But, unfortunately, there's *a lot* about Mr. Bankman he *doesn't* want you to know. Skeletons in his closet that he desperately wants to keep secret. Why? Because if they ever became known to the masses, his image would be critically tarnished. And more than anything else, Mr. Bankman wants to protect his reputation.

Some of these shameful skeletons are of Mr. Bankman's own doing; others are beyond his control. But regardless, he'd prefer that you never saw a single one, that they'd stay hidden, known only to an elite few. But unhappily for him, a bright light is about to shine on these dark recesses.

What are these skeletons he's so desperate to hide?

Let's take a look.

Skeleton No. 1 – Banks are *not* in the savings business

You may think banks are intended to be a wonderful storehouse for your money, but they're not. You see, banks are really not in the savings business at all – they're in the *lending* business. However, they need *your* capital, *your* cash, to turn around and lend to business owners and homebuyers. That's where Mr. Bankman makes his *real* money – turning your single dollar into many more – called fractional reserve banking. But he needs *your* money to do it.

However, as you know, Mr. Bankman does offer places for you to save and storehouse your money. Vehicles like CDs, money market funds, and savings accounts. But have you seen those rates lately? If not, take a look at the results from the search I ran as I was writing this chapter, searching for the *best performing* CDs in the country[i]:

BANK	1 YR CD RATE
Bank A	1.01%
Bank B	1.00%
Bank C	1.00%
Bank D	1.00%
Bank E	0.95%

Bank A captured the top spot and actually boasted a tagline reading "High Yield CD." High yield? Seriously? At 1.01 percent? I'm sure the only reason it received this moniker was because it offered 1/100th of a percentage point more than the other banks on this list. Do you even know how to calculate 1/100th of a percentage point? It translates to .0001. In other words, this additional return, which apparently allowed *Bank A* the right to say it had a *"High Yield* CD," nets the investor an additional *1 cent per year on every $100 invested*. Yeehaw! One cent! Let's throw a party and invite everyone we know. And don't forget, these were apparently the *best* offerings in the country on that specific day, at least according to this advertisement. So it likely gets worse from there, at least for you, but definitely not for Mr. Bankman. For him, this is where it starts to get really, *really* good.

You see, Mr. Bankman takes every dollar that you deposit, upon which he currently pays you a measly 1 percent in annual interest, and turns around and creates $5 – yes 5 – through fractional reserve banking[ii]. And what does he do with these $5? He loans them out to other individuals, charging them five, six, or seven times more than he is paying you. Consider *that* profit margin. Not to mention the insane (and dangerous) amount of leverage.

Let's do the math. If Mr. Bankman were to lend out $5 at 6-percent interest for every $1 he pays out 1-percent interest, he would be making a profit of 3,000 percent! See Figure 3.1.

Mr. Bankman earns 6% interest on $5 = 30 cents

Mr. Bankman pays 1% interest on $1 = 1 cent

Mr. Bankman's profit is 3,000%

Figure 3.1

In other words, in this hypothetical example, Mr. Bankman would earn 30 cents in interest (6 percent on $5) for every 1 cent he *pays in interest* (1 percent of $1). That's a 30-to-1 profit ratio – all backed and supported by your tax dollars (ahem, I mean our national government) through the FDIC insurance program. No wonder Mr. Bankman can afford custom-tailored suits.

But, unfortunately, it gets worse from here.

Skeleton No. 2 – Your *real* return is even worse

Sorry to be the bearer of bad news, but if you have money in a certificate of deposit (CD), savings account, or money market fund, your real return (the amount you get to keep *after* taxes) is actually a lot worse than you may realize.

Why? Because interest earned in any of these vehicles is considered *taxable income*. In other words, if you are in the current top marginal tax brackets for both state (ranging from a low of 4.86

percent in North Dakota to 11 percent in Hawaii)[iii] and federal (39.6 percent beginning in 2013), then up to 50.6 percent of that wonderful 1.01 percent gain has to be paid to Uncle Sam *each year* at tax time, dropping that "High Yield CD" to a net, after-tax return of just .499 percent (or .00499) – yes, that really does mean *less than* one half of 1 percent.

So if you live in Hawaii (don't you wish), your net, after-tax, annual return would be a whopping $0.50 (yes, 50 cents) on every $100 you have inside this wonderful CD.

That's about as much excitement as a human should be allowed to experience in any given year. But the excitement doesn't stop. Keep reading.

Skeleton No. 3 – Here comes Mr. Inflation

Okay, so your 1.01 percent "*High Yield* CD" has now been chopped down to a meager .499 percent (.00499) after Mr. Taxman has taken his cut. Can it really get any worse?

Unfortunately, it can.

Even though money in a one-year bank CD nets only .50 percent (rounded) after Mr. Taxman gets paid, Mr. Inflation still hasn't joined the party. But he's about to. And if you thought Mr. Taxman was a party pooper, wait until you meet Mr. Inflation.

According to www.usinflationcalculator.com, the average inflation rate for 2011 was 3.5 percent. Take a look at the graph for the 2011 inflation rate as well as that of the previous 10 years[iv]:

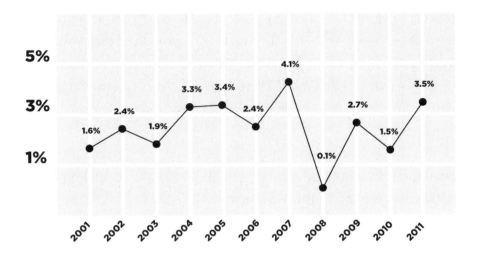

Figure 3.2

What does this mean? It means that the purchasing power of each and every dollar shrank in 2011 by 3.5 percent. In other words, what took $1 to buy in 2010 took almost $1.04 to buy in 2011. Or another way to look at it is that in 2011 your dollar only bought 96.5 cents worth of goods.

And how does this factor into your awe-inspiring "High Yield CD" that pays a stellar 1.01 percent? Well, it's not good. As a matter of fact, it's downright awful.

If this wonderful return has already been reduced by Mr. Taxman, to a net of .50 percent, and now Mr. Inflation is taking another 3.5 percent in purchasing power, that means that this wonderful "High Yield CD" is actually ***losing*** you – yes, losing you – 3 percent per year.

Did you catch that? Money in the bank is not currently *making* you anything in regard to future purchasing power. At least not at these anemic current interest rates. Rather, it is moving you *backwards* further and further and further, each and every year, thanks to the combined efforts of Mr. Bankman, Mr. Taxman, and Mr. Inflation.

So where does this leave you as a current or future retiree? If stocks are too risky for your nest egg and the bank doesn't keep you ahead of inflation, what's your answer? Well, keep on reading, because I've got some good news. Some very good news.

Chapter 4

It's What You Keep That Counts

If I were to summarize my message over the last decade into one paramount idea, it would be this – *it's not what you earn that matters; it's what you keep that counts!* And as obvious as that sounds, in my opinion it's the number-one error that most individuals make as they plan for retirement.

To help explain this concept, I'd like to tell you another story, as shared with me by one of America's top financial professionals, someone I will simply call John for the sake of this book. It's a game he likes to play during his client workshops called "It's Time to Pay Your Taxes."

Let's peek into his meeting room to see if we can get a glimpse of how this game works.

"Alright folks," John says as he pulls a wad of $1 bills out of his pocket. "We're going to play a little game. And for this game, I'm going to give you each some money."

"I knew I liked this guy," a lady whispers, as she leans close to her husband's ear.

"Here's the deal," John says. "I'm going to give each of you either $2 or $3. And I'm going to let you choose. No tricks. So raise your hand if you'd like to be part of the $3 group."

Eighty percent of the hands go up, and John's assistant, Jenny, scurries around the room doling out $3 (plus an additional small bag of coins) to each individual with his or her hand in the air.

"So the rest of you are choosing $2, correct?"

The remaining folks nod in agreement. "Now remember folks, since I'm buying dinner, I get to make the rules," John says with a smile.

A light laughter fills the room.

"I also want you to know that the numbers we will be using in this game are just averages, not exact figures. But the point of this game is to show you how the interest you earn from different types of accounts can radically affect the amount of tax you are required to pay. Remember, I told you up front that the name of this game is 'It's Time to Pay Your Taxes.'

"Okay, I'd like the people in the $3 group to raise their hands." Up shoots most of the hands in the room. "Alright, now all you greedy people can put your hands down," John says with a chuckle.

"For both groups, this money – either $2 or $3 – represents *interest* that each of you earned over the last 12 months."

One of the $2 recipients raises her hand and asks sheepishly, "Is it too late for me to change my mind? I think I'd like to be part of the $3 group." The room fills with laughter.

John, the true professional, says, "Of course not. As a matter of fact, does anyone else want to change his or her mind as well?"

Two other hands go up, and Jenny hurries around to give each of these three individuals one additional dollar.

"Alright then. Now that we've got that settled, let me tell you the *only* differences between these two groups. The first difference is obviously *how much* interest each group made. And the second difference is *where* each group earned that interest. Other than that, everything else will be exactly the same for this example."

John pauses to let those two points sink in before he continues. "Now, I want each of you to look ahead to see what's in front of you."

Sitting in front of each person is a small plastic bucket with a picture of Uncle Sam glued to it.

"What do you see?" John asks.

"Looks like a tax bucket," says one retiree.

"That's right," John says. "Remember, the name of this game is 'It's Time to Pay Your Taxes.' Here's the good news, though. Whatever money you end up with after you pay your taxes is yours to keep.

"Now, for this example, all of you make exactly the same amount of income each year – $44,000. And this $44,000 could come from many different sources – wages, interest, or even as a withdrawal from your IRA, 401(k), or other tax-qualified account. Unfortunately, though, if you receive $44,000 per year from any of these sources, once you begin receiving your Social Security checks, then the government classifies you as a 'wealthy retiree.'"

"What!?" exclaims one man in obvious frustration. "How can $44,000 make me wealthy?"

"I'm about to show you," John says. "Unfortunately, it does. At least according to the government's definition. I think it will become much clearer to you as we continue to play this game.

"Remember, other than the *amount* each group received, the

only other difference is *where* each group earned this interest. The members of the $3 group earned their annual interest in a *bank CD*, while the $2 group earned its annual interest in an *annuity*.

"So, it's now the end of the year and time to pay your taxes. If you are in the $3 group and earned this interest in a bank CD, what does the bank send you each January?"

"A 1099," someone says.

"That's right," John says. "A 1099. Or as I like to call it, an 'I'm-telling-on-you form.' Because that's exactly what it is. The bank is telling the IRS, 'Go get it boys!'

"Now let's assume, for the sake of discussion, that the $3 group pays its taxes at a total rate, both state and federal, of just 28 percent. Assuming this rate, how much would the $3 group have to pay in taxes on that $3 of interest?"

After a brief pause, one woman says, "Eighty-four cents," as she looks up from the calculator on her phone.

"That's right," John says. "Three dollars times 28 percent equals 84 cents. ($3 x 28 percent = $0.84.) But here's the big question. Are you done paying your taxes?" John asks, pausing. "Unfortunately, you're not. Remember, because you earned $3 of interest *above* the government's $44,000 limit, *you now have to pay income tax on $3 of your Social Security benefit as well* – actually on just 85 percent of the $3 you receive from Social Security, which in this case is equivalent to $2.55 (85 percent of $3). So, can someone now calculate for me what 28 percent of $2.55 equals?"

"Seventy-one cents," someone says.

"That's right. Because you are now $3 above the $44,000 income threshold, and because you earned this interest in a bank CD which issues a 1099 form, that $3 of interest income creates a *double tax* – 28-percent tax on the interest income itself *and* an *additional* 28-percent tax on $2.55 of your Social Security income. I know this might sound confusing. Sorry. Only the government could come up with this kind of craziness.

"But here's the critical thing for you to understand. The *total* tax you owe because of that measly $3 of interest is actually a whopping $1.55. So I'd like all of you that were part of the $3 group to place $1.55 in that bucket in front of you. And just in case anyone is confused, that equals one dollar, two quarters, and a nickel," John says with a laugh.

"Okay, now for the rest of you in the $2 group. Where did you earn *your* interest?"

"In an annuity," says a lady near the front of the room.

"That's right. In an annuity," John says. "And what is one of the benefits of an annuity?"

"Tax deferral?" another person asks sheepishly.

"That's right," John says again. "And guess what? *Your* $2 of interest does *not* get reported *anywhere* on your tax return simply because it was *credited* within the annuity; it also does not negatively affect your Social Security income in that year. As a matter of fact, for the current year's tax purposes, it's as if it doesn't even exist. What do you think about that?"

The lady who earlier asked to move to the $3 group blurts out, "Is it too late for me to switch back to the $2 group? I think I made a mistake."

With a glimmer in his eye, John says, "Yep. Too late. Sorry. The 1099 has already been issued."

"So folks, which group won?" John asks.

"We did," say the few people from the $2 group.

"That's right," John says. "And here's the reason why. ***It's not what you earn that matters; it's what you keep that counts.*** That one statement could change your financial future forever.

"Too many people focus only on what they can earn. But I don't care what you earn until *after* I know how it affects you tax-wise. Because *that's* the key. Does this make sense?"

The entire room nods in agreement. Each person is fully engaged.

"By the way, what tax bracket did I say all of you were in when we started this game?" John pauses for the answer. "That's right – 28 percent. But for those of you in the $3 group, do you know what I say to that? Hogwash! You just paid $1.55 on $3 of interest. That puts you in a 52-percent marginal tax bracket. Higher than the highest income earner in America! You see, the government has figured out a way to effectively put seniors and retirees into a marginal tax bracket of over 50 percent due to the *double taxation* imposed on your Social Security. What do you think about that!?"

Grumbling fills the room, and it becomes obvious that this is news to many of those in attendance.

Near the back of the room, however, sits one man who has doubt painted across his face. It's obvious he's dying to say something. Eager to catch John in a trap. Eager to prove him wrong.

But it's also clear that John reads the man's expression. He's seen this look before, and he calls him out. "Mr. Davis, I see you're giving me that look. That look that says I've forgotten something. Am I right?"

"Yes," Mr. Davis says.

"Well, I know exactly what you're thinking. Do you want to say it, or would you like me to say it first?"

Without answering John's question, Mr. Davis says, "Yeah, but the annuity group still has to pay their taxes at some point."

"Ah, so what you're *really* asking is how important is tax-deferral. Right?" John says as he clicks forward to his next slide. Up on the screen, in huge letters, is, "How important is tax deferral?"

Though Mr. Davis doesn't know it, there is a person just like him in every crowd. John is not only ready but also eager to answer this all-important question.

Chapter 5

The Magical Doubling Dollar

"Mr. Davis, I appreciate your question. Thank you. Before I answer it, though, I want to point out one very significant fact to make sure no one misses it. Remember, because interest credited within an annuity is tax deferred, it does *not* subject a retiree's Social Security benefit to *double taxation* each year when it is earned, like interest from other taxable vehicles that generate a 1099 form. That, by itself, is a huge win. Isn't it, Mr. Davis?"

"Yeah, I guess," Mr. Davis says a bit reluctantly.

"However, that wasn't your question, was it? You were really asking what difference deferring your taxes makes. Well, to illustrate this point, I want to tell you a story about 'The Magical Doubling Dollar.'"

John picks up one of the dollars out of Uncle Sam's tax bucket sitting on the table and holds it stretched tightly between both hands. "Let me ask you a question. If this dollar were to double 20 times –

$1 to $2 … $2 to $4 … $4 to $8 … $8 to $16, and so on – 20 times – how much money would you have after the 20th doubling?"

After a short period of silence, one person shouts out, "Thirty thousand dollars."

"Five million!" guesses another.

John chuckles. "Well, let's just say it's somewhere between those two guesses. The actual amount is just over $1 million – $1,048,576 to be exact."

The eyes of many in the room widen with surprise.

"Here, let me show you," John says, as he brings the following chart up on the screen.

Double 1	$2.00
Double 2	$4.00
Double 3	$8.00
Double 4	$16.00
Double 5	$32.00
Double 6	$64.00
Double 7	$128.00
Double 8	$256.00
Double 9	$512.00
Double 10	$1,024.00
Double 11	$2,048.00
Double 12	$4,096.00
Double 13	$8,192.00
Double 14	$16,384.00
Double 15	$32,768.00
Double 16	$65,536.00
Double 17	$131,072.00

Double 18	**$262,144.00**
Double 19	**$524,288.00**
Double 20	**$1,048,576.00**

Figure 5.1

"Now, let's take a look at Mr. Davis' 'Magical *Taxable* Doubling Dollar' and see how it compares. Let's take this same dollar, but instead of letting the full amount double each time, as in my example, now we are going to apply a 25-percent tax on the gain each time it doubles – not at the very end, but each and every time it doubles."

John pauses and then asks, "How much money do you think we will have at the end of the 20th doubling in this scenario? Again, assuming we apply a 25-percent tax on the gain each time it doubles?"

"Five hundred thousand!" shouts one person.

"Nope," says John. "Any more guesses?"

One person, who's clearly been trying to do the math in his head, raises his hand and says, "If the tax is 25 percent, wouldn't it be around $750,000?"

"That would be the case if you applied the tax at the very *end* of the process on the entire $1 million amount, as in the case of the annuity. But for this example, we have to apply a 25-percent tax on the gain each and every time the dollar doubles, just like what happens each year when you have to pay tax on interest from a bank CD or any other account in which you get a 1099 form," John says.

"Are you ready for the number?" John asks. "I'm glad you're sitting down because the answer to the 'Magical *Taxable* Doubling Dollar' is going to surprise you. If you had to apply a 25-percent tax on the gain each and every time this magical dollar doubled, you would end up with only $72,570."

"No way," says Mr. Davis, his expression crying foul. "It can't be that much different."

"Indeed it is," says John. "Again, let's take a look at the actual numbers."

Double 1 *less 25% of the gain* = $1.75

Double 2 *less 25% of the gain* = $3.06

Double 3 *less 25% of the gain* = $5.36

Double 4 *less 25% of the gain* = $9.38

Double 5 *less 25% of the gain* = $16.41

Double 6 *less 25% of the gain* = $28.72

Double 7 *less 25% of the gain* = $50.27

Double 8 *less 25% of the gain* = $87.96

Double 9 *less 25% of the gain* = $153.94

Double 10 *less 25% of the gain* = $269.39

Double 11 *less 25% of the gain* = $471.43

Double 12 *less 25% of the gain* = $825.01

Double 13 *less 25% of the gain* = $1,443.76

Double 14 *less 25% of the gain* = $2,526.58

Double 15 *less 25% of the gain* = $4,421.51

Double 16 *less 25% of the gain* = $7,737.64

Double 17 *less 25% of the gain* = $13,540.88

Double 18 *less 25% of the gain* = $23,696.54

Double 19 *less 25% of the gain* = $41,468.94

Double 20 *less 25% of the gain* = $72,570.64

Figure 5.2

"Folks, can you see the tremendous difference? It's amazing! Isn't it? If you applied a 25-percent tax only at the very end of the doubling period, on the full $1,048,576, you would end up with $786,432. *But*, if you have to apply that 25-percent tax to the gain each and every time the money doubles, the amount shrinks to $72,570 – less than 1/10th of the tax-deferred amount."

John now looks to the back of the room, right at Mr. Davis, who is looking less and less comfortable, and says, "So, Mr. Davis, let me ask you, does tax deferral matter?"

"Yeah, apparently it does," Mr. Davis says, a little embarrassed he ever asked the question, but happy to finally understand the truth.

Chapter 6

The Big Lie

Sometimes a lie is told so incredibly well that even those perpetrating it believe it as truth. Such is the case with stock market averages.

Let me see, how can I convey this next thought nicely, gently, in a way that doesn't offend anyone? Sorry – I can't. Here's the bitter truth. *It's a lie! Fiction. The "average" returns reported by financial companies are not reality. They're just smoke and mirrors.*

Sorry. That was as nice as I could be. It's infuriating. The sad part is that I think most of the folks in the financial industry don't understand what I'm about to tell you. And if they do, shame on them.

Here's the scoop. Most stock market indexes, as well as most mutual funds, tout their *average* returns over given periods of time – one year, three years, five years, and lifetime. They post them on their fact sheets. They share them with the media. It's what many financial professionals preach to their clients.

"Yes, Mr. Client, the S&P® 500 has returned an average of 10.64 percent over the last 20 years[v], even when you include the terrible results of both the tech crash and the credit crisis."

Baloney! That statement may be *factually* true, but in reality it's very misleading and basically worthless.

Why? Simple. There is a huge difference between the _average_ return and the _actual_ return within an account. To illustrate, I'm going to ask you a question. A question that at first glance seems ridiculously simple. Silly even. But the answer to this question could be one of the most powerful concepts you ever grasp in order to take control of your financial future. Here it is.

If a person invests $1,000 into an account, and this account experiences a negative-50-percent return in year one and a positive-50-percent return in year two, how much money would be in the account at the end of the second year?

Think about it for a second. The *average* return is zero, right?

$$\text{YEAR 1} \quad\quad \text{YEAR 2}$$
$$\frac{(-50\%) + 50\%}{2} = \frac{0}{2} = 0\% \text{ Average}$$

Figure 6.1

Well, if the average return is zero percent, then wouldn't the ending value be equal to its beginning value of $1,000?

Nope. Not even close.

The ***average*** return may be zero percent, but the ***actual*** return is negative 25 percent!

What!? How can that be?

Let me illustrate using the numbers. If a person invests $1,000 into an account, and in the first year it experiences a negative-50-percent return, then that $1,000 drops to $500, correct?

$1,000 less 50% = $500
($500)

Figure 6.2

Now, if that account has a 50-percent gain in year two, it would increase back up to $750.

$500 plus 50% = $750
($250)

Figure 6.3

So, at the end of two years, even though the average return is zero percent, the account actually experienced a 25-percent drop. And just so you don't think I rigged this equation in my favor, the results would be exactly the same if the gain was in year one and the loss was in year two.

How can this be true? If the average return is zero, how can the ending value be significantly less? Why aren't these values the same? It's very simple:

*The **"actual"** return and the **"average"** return will <u>NEVER</u> equal one another anytime you have to factor in a negative number.*

In other words, if you *ever* have to factor in a negative year's result (the year in which a market went down), then the *average* return (the number often boasted to the public) and the *actual* return (the amount that an account or fund actually experienced) will *never* be the same.

So, since markets *do* experience negative years, the averaging method just doesn't work. It will never work. It's not an accurate picture of how a market or an account has really performed; unless, of course, every year during that period has experienced a positive return. This may help you understand why your 401(k) or brokerage account balance doesn't necessarily reflect the average gains you've seen reported by the media.

What this means is that even though an investment could claim an *average* return of zero percent, as in the example above, which would be a factual statement (allowing individuals to think they haven't lost any money), the client would have experienced an actual *loss* of 25 percent of his investment.

So let's revisit that hypothetical statement made by the financial professional earlier in this chapter. "Yes, Mr. Client, the S&P® 500 has returned an average of 10.64 percent over the last 20 years." That statement would make an individual think that his accounts have *experienced* an actual annual growth of 10.64 percent. Right? Of course. What else could he think?

However, in the scenario above, the *real* return this client experienced over the last 20 years – the actual growth to his account – was only 8.82 percent[vi].

If you want to easily see these differences for yourself, I want to direct you to a great website I found called MoneyChimp.com. The site has a page, http://www.moneychimp.com/features/market_cagr.htm, on which you can enter any range of years and see the average versus the actual return. Powerful stuff.

So, why is all this important? Because by putting into practice what I am going to share with you in *Stress-Free Retirement*, and by *never* experiencing a single year with a loss, *your* average return and actual return will always be the same – always – because this strategy is contractually guaranteed to never have a negative return. *EVER*. Not in any year. No matter how much a stock (or other market) goes down. The *worst* you can do in any given year is zero. And as the saying in the industry goes, "Zero is your hero." At least when the stock market is plummeting[vii].

PART 2: THE SOLUTION

Chapter 7

Never Underestimate the Power of Zero

As I mentioned at the end of the last chapter, sometimes a zero-percent return can be your best friend. As a matter of fact, if I could give you just one piece of advice for building long-term wealth – just one – it would be this: *Never take a loss.*

Profound, huh? I know it sounds pretty basic, but those four words may be the best investment advice you ever receive. Seriously. If you followed just this one principle, you'd be *way* ahead of most of your peers. Most people in the investing world are busy chasing the next "hot" investment (like technology stocks in 1999, real estate in 2006, and gold today) when they should be simply eliminating their losses.

In this chapter I want to show you some startling, real-life examples that will illustrate just how powerful *never taking a loss* can be.

In chapter three of my second book, *The Retirement Miracle*, I show the history of one of the worst-performing major stock indexes over the last two decades – Japan's Nikkei 225 Index. Why do I use an index from Japan to illustrate the power of this concept? Is it because it in some way stacks the cards more positively in my favor for the sake of this example? No. Not at all. I use this particular index in my illustrations for one reason only – to show just how significant never taking a loss can be; and I figured that by using the worst-performing stock index (from a First World economy) I could find over the last 20 years, it would provide compelling insight. The obvious point being, if the "Power of Zero" works with *this* index, think of what it could do in markets that have not been quite so draconian.

This particular stock index, Japan's Nikkei 225, peaked over two decades ago, on December 29, 1989, at a high of 38,957.44 points. Today, as I write this chapter, that same index wallows around 8,300 points. Wow! That's a 79-percent *negative* return nearly 23 years later. See Figure 7.1 for each year's actual performance through year-end 2011.

Nikkei 225 Index's Performance from 12/31/1989 to 12/31/2011

YEAR	INDEX VALUE	GAIN OR LOSS	VALUE AT YEAR END
1989	38915.9	NA	$1,000.00
1990	23848.7	-38.72	$612.83
1991	22983.8	-3.63	$590.60
1992	16925	-26.36	$434.91
1993	17417.2	2.91	$447.56
1994	19723.1	13.24	$506.81
1995	19868.2	0.74	$510.54

1996	19361.3	-2.55	
1997	15258.7	-21.19	
1998	13842.17	-9.28	$355.0~
1999	18934.34	36.79	$486.55
2000	13785.69	-27.19	$354.24
2001	10542.6	-23.53	$270.91
2002	8578.95	-18.63	$220.45
2003	10676.6	24.45	$274.35
2004	11488.76	7.61	$295.22
2005	16111.43	40.24	$414.01
2006	17225.83	6.92	$442.64
2007	15307.78	-11.13	$393.36
2008	8859.56	-42.12	$227.66
2009	10546.44	19.04	$271.01
2010	10229	-3.01	$262.85
2011	8450	-17.39	$217.13

Figure 7.1

As you can see, this index had a positive return in 2005 that *exceeded* 40 percent. That kind of return would make anybody giddy. Unfortunately though, that's only half of the story. Even though there were some stellar gains during this 22-year time frame, the losses that followed more than wiped out the positive returns, allowing the rout to continue right through to today.

Do you recall the title of this chapter? "Never Underestimate the Power of Zero." There's a reason for that title. An important one. And in order to illustrate this title's significance, I want to show you this same chart again, but this time with one simple (*and hypothetical*) change. What if we changed each negative year's return to simply zero? In other words, no gain and no loss. Just a big, fat zero. How would that affect the results over the last 22 years? Take a look at Figure 7.2.

Nikkei 225 Index Removing All Loss Years

YEAR	INDEX VALUE	GAIN OR LOSS	VALUE AT YEAR END
1989	38915.9	NA	$1,000.00
1990	23848.7	0.00	$1,000.00
1991	22983.8	0.00	$1,000.00
1992	16925	0.00	$1,000.00
1993	17417.2	2.91	$1,029.08
1994	19723.1	13.24	$1,165.32
1995	19868.2	0.74	$1,173.90
1996	19361.3	0.00	$1,173.90
1997	15258.7	0.00	$1,173.90
1998	13842.17	0.00	$1,173.90
1999	18934.34	36.79	$1,605.74
2000	13785.69	0.00	$1,605.74
2001	10542.6	0.00	$1,605.74
2002	8578.95	0.00	$1,605.74
2003	10676.6	24.45	$1,998.36
2004	11488.76	7.61	$2,150.38
2005	16111.43	40.24	$3,015.61
2006	17225.83	6.92	$3,224.20
2007	15307.78	0.00	$3,224.20
2008	8859.56	0.00	$3,224.20
2009	10546.44	19.04	$3,838.09
2010	10229	0.00	$3,838.09
2011	8450	0.00	$3,838.09

Figure 7.2

Amazing, isn't it? By simply eliminating the losses and making them zero, the performance of this particular index went from a 79-percent *loss* to a 284-percent *gain*. And just so you don't miss what a wide margin of difference that represents, the $3,838.09 in this "no loss" scenario is 1,668 percent more money than the $217.13 in the first (and actual) example.

Now let's take this illustration one step further. What if we kept the zeros in the negative years *but lowered the gain in any single positive year to a maximum return of just 7 percent?* See Figure 7.3.

Nikkei 225 Index with No Loss Years and a 7-Percent Maximum Cap on Annual Gains

YEAR	INDEX VALUE	GAIN OR LOSS	VALUE AT YEAR END
1989	38915.9	NA	$1,000.00
1990	22983.8	0.00	$1,000.00
1992	16925	0.00	$1,000.00
1993	17417.2	2.91	$1,029.08
1994	19723.1	7.00	$1,101.12
1995	19868.2	0.74	$1,109.22
1996	19361.3	0.00	$1,109.22
1997	15258.7	0.00	$1,109.22
1998	13842.17	0.00	$1,109.22
1999	18934.34	7.00	$1,186.86
2000	13785.69	0.00	$1,186.86
2001	10542.6	0.00	$1,186.86
2002	8578.95	0.00	$1,186.86
2003	10676.6	7.00	$1,269.94
2004	11488.76	7.00	$1,358.84
2005	16111.43	7.00	$1,453.96
2006	17225.83	6.92	$1,554.53

2007	15307.78	0.00	$1,554.53
2008	8859.56	0.00	$1,554.53
2009	10546.44	7.00	$1,663.34
2010	10229	0.00	$1,663.34
2011	8450	0.00	$1,663.34

Figure 7.3

Still pretty impressive, isn't it? Even though this example *significantly limits* the gains in those few stellar years, it still provides a return that produces 667 percent *more* money than the index itself did during that same time frame, proving that there is usually more significance in protecting the downside of an account than there is in achieving huge returns.

Okay, let's take this example further still by reducing the upside potential even more. Let's see what happens during this same time period if we lower the maximum gain potential to only a 3.5-percent return in any given year. See Figure 7.4.

Nikkei 225 Index with No Loss Years and a 3.5-Percent Maximum Cap on Annual Gains

YEAR	INDEX VALUE	GAIN OR LOSS	VALUE AT YEAR END
1989	38915.9	NA	$1,000.00
1990	23848.7	0.00	$1,000.00
1991	22983.8	0.00	$1,000.00
1992	16925	0.00	$1,000.00
1993	17417.2	2.91	$1,029.08
1994	19723.1	3.50	$1,065.10
1995	19868.2	0.74	$1,072.93
1996	19361.3	0.00	$1,072.93

1997	15258.7	0.00	$1,072.93
1998	13842.17	0.00	$1,072.93
1999	18934.34	3.50	$1,110.49
2000	13785.69	0.00	$1,110.49
2001	10542.6	0.00	$1,110.49
2002	8578.95	0.00	$1,110.49
2003	10676.6	3.50	$1,149.35
2004	11488.76	3.50	$1,189.58
2005	16111.43	3.50	$1,231.22
2006	17225.83	3.50	$1,274.31
2007	15307.78	0.00	$1,274.31
2008	8859.56	0.00	$1,274.31
2009	10546.44	3.50	$1,318.91
2010	10229	0.00	$1,318.91
2011	8450	0.00	$1,318.91

Figure 7.4

Are you starting to get the picture? This hypothetical example, with extremely limited gains, still beats the actual index by a wide margin.

Okay, hang with me as I take you through one last iteration. What if we cut both the gain *and* the loss in each year to zero? In other words, what if an investor had stuck his money under his mattress or buried it in the backyard? What would he have after 22 years?

Nikkei 225 Index With No Losing Years and No Gaining Years

YEAR	INDEX VALUE	GAIN OR LOSS	VALUE AT YEAR END
1989	38915.9	NA	$1,000.00
1990	23848.7	0.00	$1,000.00
1991	22983.8	0.00	$1,000.00
1992	16925	0.00	$1,000.00
1993	17417.2	0.00	$1,000.00
1994	19723.1	0.00	$1,000.00
1995	19868.2	0.00	$1,000.00
1996	19361.3	0.00	$1,000.00
1997	15258.7	0.00	$1,000.00
1998	13842.17	0.00	$1,000.00
1999	18934.34	0.00	$1,000.00
2000	13785.69	0.00	$1,000.00
2001	10542.6	0.00	$1,000.00
2002	8578.95	0.00	$1,000.00
2003	10676.6	0.00	$1,000.00
2004	11488.76	0.00	$1,000.00
2005	16111.43	0.00	$1,000.00
2006	17225.83	0.00	$1,000.00
2007	15307.78	0.00	$1,000.00
2008	8859.56	0.00	$1,000.00
2009	10546.44	0.00	$1,000.00
2010	10229	0.00	$1,000.00
2011	8450	0.00	$1,000.00

Figure 7.5

Okay, I'm sure you saw that coming. *Of course* an account that has no gain and no loss would end up at exactly the same amount it started with, assuming there were no fees. No mystery there.

But what *is* amazing is that if a person had done simply that, never made a penny or lost a penny during this time frame, he would *still* be 361-percent *ahead* of the person who placed that money in the Nikkei 225 Index back in 1989.

So you see, it's really not so much about what you *make* in any given year as it is about making sure you never *lose*. That really *is* the key, as shown in the previous charts.

But what if you could do both?

What if you could make a positive return in the years the market was up, while at the same time never lose money in the years the market was down? That would be a real game-changer. Guess what? That's exactly what some of today's new annuities are designed to do. Let's take a look.

But before we move on to the next chapter, and look at some of those specific features, I want to point out that this study is *not* just about the Japanese economy. It has everything to do with us here in America as well. To illustrate, let's take a look at the performance of one of America's leading stock indexes, the S&P® 500, over the last 12 years.

Back on December 31, 1999, the S&P® 500 Index ended the year at 1469.25 points. Twelve years later, on December 30, 2011, that same index ended the year at 1257.60. In other words, during that 12-year period this index had a cumulative loss of 14.4 percent. To put it into tangible perspective, $100,000 placed into a fund tracking the S&P® 500 Index from December 31, 1999 through December 31, 2011 (12 years) would only be worth $85,600 and that does not take fees or inflation into account.

Let's now see how these last 12 years would have fared on an account with a beginning value of $100,000 if we could have eliminated every negative year's loss in the S&P® 500 Index during this period, even if we lowered our maximum gain to just a meager 5 percent. See Figure 7.6:

S&P® 500 Index with No Loss Years and a 5-Percent Maximum Cap on Annual Gains

YEAR	INDEX VALUE	GAIN OR LOSS	VALUE AT YEAR END
1999	1469.25	0.00	$100,000
2000	1320.28	0.00	$100,000
2001	1148.08	0.00	$100,000
2002	879.82	0.00	$100,000
2003	1111.92	5.00	$105,000
2004	1211.92	5.00	$110,250
2005	1248.29	3.00	$113,558
2006	1418.3	5.00	$119,236
2007	1468.36	3.53	$123,445
2008	903.25	0.00	$123,445
2009	1115.1	5.00	$129,617
2010	1257.64	5.00	$136,098
2011	1257.6	0.00	$136,098

Figure 7.6

Again, we see a similar result as with the Nikkei 225 Index. By eliminating our losses (even with reducing our *maximum* gain to only 5 percent) we end this 12-year period with a cumulative 36.1-percent **gain** instead of a 14.4-percent **loss**. That represents 59 percent *more* money.

Now, I'll be the first to say that no one – and I mean *no one* – knows what the next 12, or 20, or 50 years hold in store for the markets. Only time will tell us that. However, regardless of what the markets do, I believe protecting your downside is ***the*** key to long-term success.

I spoke with a financial professional recently who was asked by one of his customers how much he should put into a strategy like this. His reply was, "Only as much as you want to get back."

So let's take a look at the product that can make this possible, a product called a Fixed Indexed Annuity.

Chapter 8

The Fixed Indexed Annuity – A High Level View

I'm not a puzzle guy, but many of my relatives were as I was growing up. They loved them. One-thousand-piece puzzles. Three-thousand-piece puzzles. The bigger the better. And every holiday, off in a corner, stood the familiar green, vinyl-topped card table littered with thousands of pieces you needed a microscope to see. Around this table stood four matching vinyl chairs, inviting all to take a turn at that season's new project.

Since I never saw the point of puzzles, even as a kid, I rarely took my turn at the four chairs. (I mean, why spend all that time putting a picture *back* together? Someone should have just kept it together in the first place.) However, I *would* often help an aunt or uncle sort out all of the pieces into the bottom and top lid of the puzzle box. All of the flat-edged outside pieces went into the decorative box top, while the jagged, center pieces went into the boring, brown, lower half. I remember asking my aunt once why we needed to separate the pieces, and she said, "Because it's a lot easier to complete a puzzle if you connect all the outside edges first. It gives you a starting place and a frame of reference for the entire picture."

I think that's a good analogy for this chapter. The next few pages are not intended to complete the entire picture of the Fixed Indexed Annuity any more than the edges of a puzzle. However, they *will* give you a solid and workable foundation for what's to come.

Think of this as your 30,000-foot vantage point. Staring out the plane's window, if you will, onto the Fixed Indexed Annuity's expansive landscape, like the patchwork quilt of fields you see flying over Texas, Oklahoma, or Iowa. A shape and an outline with little definition. But also know this is simply our starting point. We will spend some time in a few of these fields, up close and personal.

However, before I begin, let me give you a very general definition. Simply put, a Fixed Indexed Annuity ("FIA" as we'll refer to it) is an insurance product designed to protect your life's savings. A tax-deferred, long-term financial tool designed for growth and safety, especially for those who are fed up with the sleepless nights that stock market volatility creates. It is also one of the few exclusive retirement vehicles that has the ability to *guarantee* (based on the claims-paying ability of the insurance company) an income stream for life – an income you cannot outlive.

Okay, that's more like the view from outer space. Now let's come back down to our 30,000-foot view and take a look at nine unique features this product offers. I think some of these will really surprise you.

1. FIAs Provide Tax Deferral

Just as we learned in John's game, "It's Time to Pay Your

Taxes," interest *credited* within an annuity is NOT reportable to the IRS and therefore does not get taxed each and every year simply because it is *credited*, as it does within taxable accounts. Also, because it doesn't get taxed when it is credited, but rather when it is withdrawn, the simple fact of receiving it doesn't subject a retiree's Social Security benefits to the destructive penalty of double taxation discussed in chapter four.

I cannot stress the significance of this point enough. It's huge. Not only will the money inside of the annuity grow much faster but it can potentially save hundreds, if not thousands, of dollars in excessive Social Security taxation.

2. FIAs Provide Insurance for Your Nest Egg

It's important to understand that, at its core, an annuity is an insurance policy. An insurance policy for your life's savings. Prior to the more recent generation of annuities, like the FIA, the primary function of an annuity was to insure a person from outliving his or her income. And while that's still one of the many valuable features of any annuity, the feature that excites me most about the FIA, especially in the current market environment, is the opportunity to insure a retiree's nest egg against loss. In short, a Fixed Indexed Annuity is "Nest Egg Insurance."

One of my favorite analogies throughout the years has been this question. If you owned a $400,000 house free and clear, and the bank didn't force you to buy homeowner's insurance, would you still buy the insurance? In other words, would you spend a few hundred dollars a year to make sure you could replace one of your biggest assets if it was destroyed by fire or some other peril? Of course you would!

Yet at the same time, many individuals leave their entire life's savings completely exposed to the risk of loss with no thought to protection. And the only reason I can think of as to why they would do this is because they simply don't know that protection exists, especially protection coupled with the opportunity for gain. Well, it does, and you're about to discover the good news.

3. FIAs Provide Upside Potential with No Downside Market Risk

I want to explain in full detail how this is possible, and will do so in chapter 10, because it's one of those aspects that just seems a little too good to be true. But, fortunately, it's not. It's fact – based on pure math. And once you understand the mechanics, it makes perfect sense. But for this brief section, I simply want you to know that this type of product *does* exist. With a Fixed Indexed Annuity, you are able to participate in a portion of a market index's gains during its positive years, but at the same time, never sustain a loss during its negative years. Again, you'll get the full explanation in chapter 10.

4. FIAs Generally Charge No Annual Management Fee

In its basic form, without optional policy additions, called riders, a Fixed Indexed Annuity generally does not charge any annual management fee or expense to the owner. In other words, there is no annual 1-percent or 2-percent drawdown of a client's total account. In my opinion, the FIA cost structure is one that puts the client's interests above the financial professional's pocketbook, and that is *always* the proper order.

Sure, individuals selling Fixed Indexed Annuities *do* make a commission, but that money generally gets paid in a *one-time,* up-front, lump-sum commission and is not an ongoing percentage of the client's total portfolio value. This alone can make a huge difference over the course of a 30- or 40-year investment horizon, but the best news is this. And hear this clearly. **With all reputable companies I know, the insurance agent's commission does NOT get subtracted from the amount the client puts into his or her annuity; rather, it is paid directly to the agent from the insurance company's general funds and profits.**

Do you understand what this means? It means that if a client puts $100,000 into a Fixed Indexed Annuity, without optional riders, she **still** has the full $100,000 in her annuity, even after the agent's commission has been paid.

But it gets even better. A lot better. Take a look at No. 5.

[Note: While the FIA generally does *not* assess an ongoing sales or management fee to the client each year, it does generally have a surrender charge that lasts for a certain number of years (varying by state and product). However, this surrender charge is generally assessed only on amounts withdrawn *above* the Penalty-Free Withdrawal allowed within most Fixed Indexed

Annuities. More on this in later chapters.]

5. FIAs Usually Pay an Initial Deposit Bonus

If not having to deduct a commission out of your contribution was exciting, then you're *really* going to love this next feature. Many Fixed Indexed Annuities actually pay the client a *BONUS* on the initial purchase amount. This bonus can fluctuate based on many different factors, but as of this writing, most bonuses tend to range between 2 and 10 percent. (Again, this is both state and product specific. Ask a licensed, local representative to find out what's available in your state.)

This means that a client who buys a $100,000 Fixed Indexed Annuity with a 10-percent bonus will have an immediate account balance (though not all immediately accessible) of $110,000*. Yes, that's right. A $10,000 *ledger* gain from day one. Wow! Think of that.

In my first book, *Tax-Free Retirement,* I refer to certain types of money as "Free Money," and I think this fits that definition quite nicely. And my belief remains the same as it did back then – when given the chance, take *all* the "Free Money" you can get!

* Please note that some bonuses may be subject to a recapture schedule for early surrender or withdrawal. Also, in some cases, bonuses may also effect features including, but not limited to, surrender charges, surrender periods, and cap rates.

6. FIAs Offer Penalty-Free Withdrawals

Generally, once an FIA has been in force for 12 months, the owner is allowed to take a Penalty-Free Withdrawal. While the amount allowed for withdrawal can vary from company to company, it's fairly common within the industry to see a 10-percent withdrawal provision per year.

What I love about this feature is that in most cases it usually provides the necessary liquidity the client desires without having to be charged a direct, ongoing, annual fee.

I think it's also important to point out that in some cases FIAs allow the owner access beyond the Penalty-Free Withdrawal amount for such things as nursing home costs and other medical emergencies. As with any special, non-standard feature, which will vary by state, I suggest you get in touch with a local professional to discuss your specific situation.

7. FIAs Can Provide Guaranteed Lifetime Income

While this can be one of the most powerful and beneficial aspects of all annuities, it is also one of the most misunderstood. I believe this misunderstanding may be one of the leading reasons annuities wrongly fall under perennial attack from some in the financial community, especially those under-informed television and radio personalities. It's an amazing and powerful feature, but one whose benefits are greatly misperceived.

An FIA, in its basic form, is an accumulation vehicle used to build a nest egg. And, in many cases, that is all the annuity is intended to do – grow bigger and bigger and provide a pot of money in the future that the individual can utilize in whatever form or fashion he or she desires.

However, for those to whom an annual income is of highest importance, FIAs, and annuities in general, provide a very valuable feature – the ability to turn the entire pot of accumulated money into a lifetime stream of income. An income they *cannot* outlive, much like the pensions of yesteryear.

And while this option is extremely beneficial to those whose primary need is income, it is *never mandatory*. It is simply an option. But a very powerful and significant option. However, if a client simply wants to keep full access and control of his entire pot of money he is welcome to do so. This income feature is totally elective and never needs to be chosen unless it is desired and best fits the client's specific needs.

8. Most FIAs Lock In Credited Interest

If an FIA had a "special sauce," this would be *IT* – the Reset Provision. This provision not only protects the annuity owner's original premium amount from any market losses, it also protects *all interest* that is credited to the account as well. In other words, once interest has officially been credited to the FIA, it becomes protected, just like the original premium.

Remember the story about Judy in chapter two? Remember why she told David she was so thrilled at her two-year review? It wasn't just because she hadn't lost a single penny as the stock market was plummeting, but also because she still saw the 17-percent gain from the previous year in her account as well.

You see, once interest is credited to an FIA that offers the Reset Provision, it's always protected. And that is one *sweet* "special sauce!"

9. FIAs Can Offer Avoidance of Probate

This one is simple. Because an annuity is an insurance contract with listed beneficiaries, just like a life insurance policy, it generally pays the benefit owed to the beneficiary very quickly, without being involved in the long, arduous, and expensive task of having to struggle through probate. This allows heirs and other beneficiaries to receive money within days or weeks instead of months or years. And that can make a major difference.

So there you have it, a thumbnail sketch of some of the Fixed Indexed Annuity's unique features. But remember, this is neither a detailed nor exhaustive list. It's simply intended to give you an overview of some of the powerful benefits provided and a sneak peek into what's to come.

Chapter 9

What A Fixed Indexed Annuity is *Not*

In the last chapter, I gave you a high-altitude view of nine primary features provided by a Fixed Indexed Annuity. However, I thought it would be equally helpful to explain what a Fixed Indexed Annuity is *not*.

First, a Fixed Indexed Annuity (FIA) is *not* a get-rich-quick scheme. You should not enter this product thinking you are going to see a 20- or 30-percent return. Nor should you plan for the 17-percent return that Judy experienced in chapter two. While those years *could* happen on a very rare occasion, especially if you pick the right product, they are definitely an anomaly. Rather, FIAs are designed to provide an alternative to other fixed investments.

Before I go on to the next topic, though, I want to address something that should be obvious to all, though unfortunately is not, in regard to *get-rich-quick* ideas in general. Simply put, there is no such thing. A dependable way to get-rich-quick does not exist. Trust me on this. *Get-**poor**-quick* opportunities abound. But *get-**rich**-quick* opportunities are a myth. The only way to build wealth – real wealth – is to do so slowly, steadily, and wisely. Please don't let anyone convince you otherwise, no matter how compelling the story, or you will find yourself licking your wounds for years to come.

Here's the second thing an FIA is not. It is *not* a suitable product for a person who wants or needs access to most of his or her money within a couple years of the initial purchase. This is a longer-term strategy. Now "longer-term" can mean different things to different people, but the most common lengths of contract terms for FIAs are five, seven, and 10 years. Of course, surrenders and withdrawals *can* be made *prior* to those time periods. As I mentioned in the last chapter, most contracts allow up to a 10-percent, Penalty-Free Withdrawal per year after the first 12 months. But beyond that amount, an individual could experience a surrender charge on excess withdrawals.

Here's what one financial professional says on this subject:

"Annuities offer a wonderful option called a Penalty-Free Withdrawal (PFW). And the Penalty-Free Withdrawal is just that, allowing annuity owners the ability to withdraw funds from their account without incurring the normal surrender charge. Now, these amounts vary in size, but most companies commonly allow withdrawals of up to 10 percent of the base annuity value each year, beginning in year two. For example, if a person had a base annuity value of $100,000 in a contract that allowed the standard 10-percent PFW, he could withdraw $10,000 each year without incurring any penalty or surrender charge from the annuity company, usually beginning in year two.

"It is important to note, however, that the annuity owner will be responsible for any taxes that may be due on the withdrawal of funds, as well as the additional IRS penalty of 10 percent on any gain withdrawn if the owner is younger than 59½ years old. (Please check with a local CPA for all of your tax questions and concerns.)

"But this unique Penalty-Free Withdrawal feature is music to the ears of most retirees who have rolled funds from an IRA or 401(k) into a Fixed Indexed Annuity. Why? Because very few individuals would ever withdraw more than 10 percent from their account in any given year anyway, so the PFW usually makes the surrender charge a non-issue for most individuals. And once their money is in an FIA, they know it's safe from stock market loss. And that often brings complete peace of mind to today's retiree."

Good words. I couldn't agree more.

And last, but not least, here's the third thing an FIA is not. It is *not* a high-fee financial product. Without a doubt, this is the most misunderstood aspect of a Fixed Indexed Annuity. And while I will cover this issue in great detail in chapter 14, I'd like you to hear another representative's thoughts on this topic as well.

"It's amazing how frequently I have individuals come back to my office after our initial meeting, regurgitating the comments heard from their current representative. Comments like, 'This guy is only trying to sell you an FIA because he gets a big commission.' *Nothing could be further from the truth.* I always find this claim to be so ridiculous that it's laughable. I mean, seriously? Aren't these the same people who charge their clients fees of 1 percent to 2 percent *each and every year*, even when they are losing their clients' money? FIA agents like me get paid a commission one time. And none of it comes from the client's account. Rather, it is paid out of the issuing insurance company's pockets."

This individual continues: "I always wonder why a financial professional would bring up an annuity agent's compensation when *none* of it is actually paid out of the client's funds in the first place.

On the surface it doesn't make any sense. But when you look a little deeper it does. The reason other professionals like to make such claims is because they are simply trying to scare the client from moving his or her money. It's that simple. It's a scare tactic. And a false one at that. I like to ask the individual if I can call his or her current representative right then so we can wander back into a land called reality.

"It's critically important for the client to understand that the annuity agent's entire commission gets paid by (and from) the issuing insurance company, and *not* from his or her annuity premium. It *in no way* diminishes or reduces the annuity value. Now, when we compare this to the 1-2 percent in average annual fees charged by many other financial representatives, which **does get paid directly from the client's funds**, it makes their argument utterly ridiculous. Most clients working with this other type of representative will pay between 10 percent and 20 percent, and sometimes more, **from their own account value** over that same 10-year time period. And once again, when a client purchases an FIA, *none* of that commission comes from the client's funds. So I always wonder, is this expense issue *really* a debate a competing financial representative wants to have with me in front of his client?"

So let's recap. Here are three things a Fixed Indexed Annuity is *not*.

1. It is *not* a get-rich-quick scheme.
2. It is *not* a good place for short-term money.
3. It is *not* a high-fee financial vehicle.

Chapter 10

How Can They Do That?

People often ask me the same question you likely have running through your mind at this very moment: "How can any company afford to let your money increase when a particular market goes up without making you participate in that market's losses as well?" It just seems too good to be true; but fortunately, it's not. It's very real and very possible.

If you're familiar with the many different terms in the financial universe then you have likely heard of a financial tool called an "option." However, you may not know what an option actually is or how it works.

An option is simply a tool that allows a person to profit from the *direction* of a market. If a person owns an option, he or she doesn't own any particular underlying stock or commodity. Rather, the option owner is simply betting on (and will make a profit or loss from) the *direction* of a market movement.

There are two basic types of options: Puts and calls.

Those who own a *put option* make a profit when a market goes *down*. Those who own a *call option* make a profit when a market goes *up*. In its basic form, it really is that simple.

So here's how all this works together. When a client purchases a Fixed Indexed Annuity, the vast majority of his or her annuity premium goes to purchase a solid, balanced, and diversified bond portfolio. Because this bond portfolio generally produces a return based on interest rates, it's predictable and carries little to no stock or commodity market risk. It will produce the same rate of interest regardless of whether these markets go up or down.

However, not all of the annuity premium goes into the bond portfolio. A very small portion of the client's annuity premium also goes to purchase call options on the index that the annuity is tracking. If this particular index, such as the S&P® 500, goes up, these call options exponentially increase in value, allowing the insurance company to credit interest based on some of those gains, usually up to a set "cap" amount, or maximum. And if the market these options are tracking goes down, the small amount of money used to purchase the options expires worthless, much like the premium you might pay for auto insurance in a year you don't have an accident. And, even in a losing year, the cost to purchase that option by the insurance company is soon recouped by the income that is produced from the diversified bond portfolio.

Simply put, bonds provide the downside protection, and options provide the upside growth potential.

None of your money is actually invested in that particular market the FIA is tracking – and that is why you have no actual market risk. This is critically important (and exciting) to understand.

Does this make sense? I hope so. If nothing else, just know that this strategy is not some mystical leap of faith, but rather a predictable set of calculations prepared by some of the world's most talented mathematicians[viii].

Chapter 11

The Powerful Income Rider

So far in this book you've witnessed the power of the FIA as an accumulation tool. Now I want to show you one of the additional options available, called an Income Rider. While the Income Rider may not be for everyone, it is an incredibly powerful feature, especially for those who desire future income. Of course, since this provides an additional benefit, it does come with a small additional cost.

And please also know that what is described in this chapter is very general in nature. It in no way depicts how every Income Rider works. Far from it. But as you might imagine, there is a high degree of overlap and similarity, and it's this commonality that I'd like to discuss in these next few pages. And I think the best way to accomplish this is through a hypothetical question-and-answer session between client and insurance agent.

Let's listen in.

Client: What exactly is an Income Rider?

Agent: An Income Rider, simply put, is a feature that can guarantee a lifetime stream of income, usually based upon a pre-determined, guaranteed rate of return, regardless of actual annuity performance.

Client: I understand what you mean by a lifetime stream of income, but what do you mean by a guaranteed rate of return, regardless of actual annuity performance?

Agent: This is where a lot of confusion exists in the marketplace. A Fixed Indexed Annuity, which includes an Income Rider, actually has two different ledger balances to keep track of. One of these ledgers is the surrender value – the amount of money you can actually withdraw from your annuity.

The Income Rider, on the other hand, does not work this way. This ledger balance can increase in value *even when the index is negative.* It is a way in which insurance companies offer the client some level of positive interest, every year, regardless of the actual index performance within that particular FIA. *But here's the catch,* to receive this potentially higher value, the client cannot access the entire lump sum of money at his discretion; but rather, he must choose to receive this higher value through a series of annual income payments. Unlike the annuity surrender value – which is entirely your money to do with as you please (less any surrender charges that may still be in force) – you cannot access the entire Income Rider value as a lump sum. It must be taken in annual payments, similar to a pension.

Let me give you an example of how this Income Rider might work. Let's say Paul buys a $100,000 annuity that grows at an average of 5 percent per year over a 10-year period. At the end of those 10 years, assuming Paul had taken no withdrawals, his annuity would be worth $162,889. Assuming there were no surrender charges in force after 10 years, which is generally the case with most of today's FIAs, Paul would have full access to the entire $162,889. He can access that full amount, either in part, or in whole, any time he wishes.

Before we look at the potential Income Rider value in this scenario, I must first tell you there are two primary methods in which insurance companies apply the increase in value to this rider. The first is a "set interest rate" approach, and the other is what is called a "stacking" method. Let's first look at how the "set interest rate" approach works.

With the set interest rate type of Income Rider, the *ledger value* is guaranteed to increase every year based upon a predetermined rate of interest. For instance, if an insurance company offered a 6-percent Income Rider on its FIA, that would mean this Income Rider's *ledger value* would increase every year by 6 percent – regardless of how the annuity itself actually performed. So, in this example, a 6-percent growth over this same 10-year period would result in an Income Rider ledger balance of $179,085 – $16,196 more than the actual FIA surrender value. *But* – and this is a *big but* – the client does not actually have $179,085 he or she can withdraw from the annuity. This higher value can *only* be realized if the client chooses to take a stream of income.

But here's the critical part to understand. ***The client always has the choice!*** If the values are close, as in the example above, the client may choose to never exercise the Income Rider benefit, but rather choose to keep full access and control of the entire pot of money, just as in any other account.

However, let's say due to poor market performance, this same annuity only increased by 2 percent annually over that same 10-year period. In this example, Paul's surrender value would only be worth $121,899 at the end 10 years. Not great. But if he received a 6-percent guarantee on his Income Rider, then that rider's ledger value would still be worth $179,085 at the end of 10 years. In this case, because the Income Rider value is so much higher than the actual base annuity value, it might make tremendous sense for Paul to choose to take his money as a stream of income, because it would give him access to that stream of income based upon a value that was $57,186 (47 percent) higher than his surrender value.

Earlier, I mentioned that there is a great amount of confusion regarding this feature. Let me explain what I mean by that. Many agents will *erroneously tell consumers* that an FIA will guarantee the consumer a certain growth, like 6 percent. This is simply not the case. What they are referring to is the Income Rider guarantee, *not the growth of the annuity itself,* so it should never be stated in this manner. This can be terribly misleading.

Client: You mentioned there were two ways to credit the growth of the Income Rider. What is the second way?

Agent: The other way is actually my favorite method. It's newer and more progressive. It's called a "stacking" Income Rider. With this method, the Income Rider simply guarantees its value will grow by the actual annuity performance **plus** an additional set interest rate added *on top* of that performance.

Let's look at another example. Let's see how a stacking 4-percent Income Rider might perform using the same 5-percent actual annuity performance from the previous example. If the base annuity grew by an annual average of 5 percent over a 10-year period, it would be worth $162,889 as we mentioned in the first example. However, since this annuity offered a stacking Income Rider, and not a set interest rate Income Rider, this rider's ledger value after 10 years would be $236,736 – a 9-percent annual appreciation. Why? Because this type of stacking Income Rider guarantees that its value will always be the actual annuity performance *plus* the guaranteed stacking interest rate – in this case an *additional* 4 percent.

Just to clarify this a little further, if this annuity had grown an average of only 2 percent per year during this time period, the Income Rider ledger would have grown by 6 percent – again, it's the base annuity growth (2 percent) plus the additional 4 percent that the rider provides stacked on top. Conversely, if the annuity had grown an average of 8 percent per year, the Income Rider ledger value would grow by 12 percent.

But not until the client is ready to withdraw his money does he need to decide whether he would prefer to have access to his full annuity surrender value or whether he would prefer to have the Income Rider value, paid through an ongoing series of annual income payments.

Does this make sense?

Client: Yes it does. But this kind of benefit sounds like it would be very expensive. How much does something like this cost?

Agent: Many Income Riders cost between 0.5 percent and 1.5 percent annually, which is generally taken out of the base value of the annuity. Of course, there are exceptions to this, but that's a pretty good rule of thumb.

Client: This may sound like a silly question, but why wouldn't everyone add the Income Rider to their FIA?

Agent: That's a very good question, actually. While it can serve individuals who want a guaranteed lifetime income very well, that is certainly not everybody's goal. First, since there is an additional cost involved, the performance of the base annuity will be reduced by the cost of the Income Rider fee each year. And if an individual is not interested in turning this pot of money into a stream of income payments sometime in the future, then this benefit would not be worth the added cost. However, with the increased guarantees that the Income Rider provides, even though it's received through annual income payments, I think it makes sense for most people to at least take a look at it. It could come in very handy, especially since no one knows for sure what his or her future financial situation will be in 10 or 20 years.

The second reason not everyone would add this rider to an FIA is that they are not allowed to do so based on their age. They may be too young or they may be too old. Most FIAs have age restrictions that need to be met in order to add this rider to the annuity.

But short of those two reasons, I think most individuals should take a good hard look at adding this rider, because it can provide a tremendous benefit to today's retiree.

Client: So how do we know if adding this rider is a good idea for us or not?

Agent: That's easy. Meet with a local and knowledgeable insurance agent. One who specializes in these products and knows your personal needs, desires, and goals. Only then can he or she advise you on the best options for your specific situation.

Client: Just a couple more questions. What happens to the income stream I'm receiving when I've reached the total amount within my annuity?

Agent: This is one of the huge benefits of the Income Rider. It transfers your risk of outliving your income to the insurance company. You no longer have to carry that burden upon your own shoulders. Why? Because if you utilize the payout of the Income Rider, you simply cannot outlive your income. Even once you've received payments far in excess of your base annuity value, the insurance company will keep paying you that annual income, for as long as you live.

However, another question I frequently get asked is, "What if I die too soon, before I have received income payments that equal the base value?" I have good news for you there as well. If you die prior to the annual income payments exhausting the base value within your annuity, then the remaining account balance will usually be passed on to your beneficiary at the time of your death.

Client: When I use an Income Rider, do I give up my entire pot of money forever? In other words, is using the benefit of the Income Rider the same thing as annuitization?

Agent: No it's not. An income stream generated by an Income Rider is not the same thing as annuitization. Annuitization occurs when a policy owner exchanges the lump sum value of his or her annuity for a lifetime income stream; and this choice cannot be reversed. With an Income Rider, however, that decision can usually be reversed. The owner (or heirs upon death) *can* still receive the base annuity value, however it would be less the amount that the Income Rider had already paid out, of course.

Client: Thank you. That's very interesting. Now for the important question. When's your next availability, so we can have you look at our current situation?

Agent: As they say, "There's no time like the present." Let's take a look.

Chapter 12

Taking off the Lid –

The Power of an *UNCAPPED STRATEGY*

I hope the amazing potential for safe growth, talked about in the last few chapters, gets your heart pounding like Secretariat's down the backstretch. Just think. You no longer have to choose between the two, standard, pathetic options: Stock market risk *or* anemic growth. Now you can have both the benefits of zero stock market risk *and* the potential for a robust, tax-deferred growth. You really *can* have your proverbial cake and eat it, too. But now I'm going to ice that cake with the sweetest frosting you've ever tasted. The frosting of an *Uncapped Strategy*.

This concept is as difficult to find in the annuity marketplace as a bald dude in a barber's chair. As a matter of fact, not long ago, it was *more* than difficult to find. It was *impossible* to find. Why? Because it simply didn't exist. But as of this writing, it *does* exist, though not with many companies.

What does an *Uncapped Strategy* mean? How can it benefit you? Glad you asked ... and I hope you're sitting down.

To illustrate how an *Uncapped Strategy* works, let's take a look at the S&P® 500 Index over the same 12-year period that we looked at in chapter seven – 1999 through 2011. (*Please note, this S&P® 500 example illustrating the power of the Uncapped Strategy is simply a hypothetical teaching tool for the purposes of this book. It is not indicative of any specific product nor any product's actual performance.*)

Back in chapter seven, I explained how $100,000 tracking the S&P® 500 Index from December 31, 1999 (when it closed at 1469.25) until December 30, 2011 (when it closed at 1257.60) would have resulted in a loss of 14.4 percent, leaving that individual with only $85,600.

I then showed you that if we eliminated the five losing years – even if we capped our maximum gain in any single year to just 5 percent – that individual would have ended that 12-year period with $136,098, or a 36.1-percent gain instead of a 14.4-percent loss.

But here's what I didn't show you. What if we could still eliminate all five of those losing years, making them zero, but keep *all* of the gains, the full amount, in the positive years. This is where it gets incredibly exciting. And this is what an *Uncapped Strategy* is all about. Take a look at Figure 12.1.

1999	1469.25	NA	$100,000
2000	1320.28	0.00	$100,000
2001	1148.08	0.00	$100,000
2002	879.82	0.00	$100,000
2003	1111.92	26.38	$126,380
2004	1211.92	8.99	$137,742
2005	1248.29	3.00	$141,874
2006	1418.30	13.62	$161,197

2007	1468.36	3.53	$166,887
2008	903.25	0.00	$166,887
2009	1115.10	23.45	$206,022
2010	1257.64	12.78	$232,352
2011	1257.60	0.00	$232,352

Figure 12.1

Wow! Do you see this! If an individual had simply been able to eliminate the five losing years in that 12-year period, while at the same time keeping the full gains in the seven positive years, he would have ended up with $232,352 – $146,752 more money – or 171-percent greater value in the account.

It really is a remarkable difference. Isn't it?

Well, you know what? In its simplest form, **THAT IS** the basic definition of an *Uncapped Strategy*. It's the ability to have unlimited gains in the positive years while, at the same time, eliminating all of the losses in the negative years.

Crazy? Absolutely. But crazy good *and* completely achievable. So here's the million-dollar question. ***If you could receive unlimited upside potential without the fear of market loss, why would you want to accumulate money through any other method?***

Seriously. Pause for a moment and think about that.

Now, please hear me. I'm not saying you *shouldn't* accumulate money through other methods. Nor am I saying this is the only product you should own. Diversity can be good. (As long as you're not just diversifying losses.) I'm simply asking, *Why would you want to accumulate money anywhere else?* It's a question you might need to wrestle with for a few days before you realize that, maybe, the real obstacle to this incredible new opportunity has simply been misinformation or, possibly, a complete lack of knowledge that these strategies even exist. Luckily, though, that's no longer an issue. Thank goodness.

PART 3: BRINGING IT ALL TOGETHER

Chapter 13

What is it *YOU* Want?

So as a retiree (or prospective retiree) what is it **you** want?

Do you want the ability to grow your money safe and secure without ridiculous fees and expenses? Great. I don't know a more powerful tool than the Fixed Indexed Annuity.

Do you want to secure an income that is guaranteed to last your entire lifetime? Perfect. That's exactly what an FIA is designed to provide.

Or do you want to pass money to the next generation without the hassle and delay of probate? Awesome. There are few better ways.

If one of these three ideas captures your interest, then I'm going to encourage you to do one important thing – take action! Now. Today. Nothing is going to happen if you simply let this information sit passively on the page in black and white. To improve your current circumstances, to eliminate the fear of volatility, and to remove the pain of market losses, you must *do something*. And if you're not getting the investment results you've been hoping for, then it seems pretty obvious that you must do something *different*. However, the ball is in your court. It's your call. Take the next step, and check it out. You'll never know how bright your future can be until you do.

Chapter 14

What About the Fees?

Centuries ago, educated and grown adults believed the world was flat. Ludicrous, isn't it? Yet that was a firmly held belief until 540 B.C., when a Greek philosopher and mathematician named Pythagoras clearly articulated that the world was *not* flat, but rather spherical in shape. It shocked the masses. Wrecked their paradigms. A staunchly held belief was obliterated by fact. (Funny how that happens.)

And so it is in the financial world. There are many "flat-earth" theories that are just plain false.

One of these common misperceptions resides in the annuity world – the false belief that annuities are expensive to own. Or that they carry high fees. This is simply a "flat-earth" theory. It may have been true of products from years gone by, but today it is definitely not the case, at least in regard to Fixed Indexed Annuities. And just like Pythagoras changed people's thinking 2,500 years ago, I want to expose the facts of today's annuity marketplace so the truth can be revealed.

Now I'm certainly not going to go down in history as changing the world with this revelation, but I am hoping that I can at least help change *your* financial future.

Simply put, Fixed Indexed Annuities are *not* expensive to own. As a matter of fact, unless additional benefits are chosen, often referred to as riders, there is usually *no* initial sales charge and *no* annual management fee at all. None. Zilch. Nada. Zippo.

So tell me. How can something that subtracts nothing from a client's account on an annual basis be considered expensive?

Good question.

Not only do most Fixed Indexed Annuities *not* have an initial sales charge or annual management fee (unless a rider is chosen), but they generally pay a **deposit bonus** to the purchaser – usually ranging from 2 to 10 percent on the *initial*, first-year premium paid, depending on the state in which the client lives and the product that is selected.

So why all of the heartburn and misinformation? I wish I knew. I can, however, offer a couple of theories. One possibility is that it's simply a carry-over from the annuities of decades past, which *did* carry hefty charges and fees. The early "ancestors" of the products we have today. But let me tell you, evolution has been very kind to the annuity species, because today's FIA, in my opinion, is better than its predecessors in almost every way.

The second possibility is, once again, the misinformation perpetuated by many in the financial marketplace. If this false label of "expensive" is being espoused simply so the financial professional can acquire the client's money under his management, then that is completely unethical, in my opinion. Just plain wrong. No financial professional should ever suggest that any individual pursue a certain course of action based on the representative's pocketbook; rather, he or she should *always* educate the client and encourage that individual to do what is best for his or her own personal and unique needs. Always. Without exception. Even if that advice results in sending that client to a different professional who *does* offer the proper products and tools to meet that individual's needs. Is that a difficult thing to do? Absolutely. But I have always believed that doing the right thing for every client, every time – including referring them to a different professional, if necessary – is not only the best way to conduct business, it's the *only* way to conduct business.

However, the good news is that during my travels, the vast majority of the professionals I have met in the financial industry are kind, well-intentioned, and honest individuals who want nothing less than the absolute best for their clients. To do what's right for each and every one. Therefore, I am going to assume that any of these individuals who make the blanket statement that "annuities are expensive" simply lack the full and proper understanding of the product. But regardless, hopefully these few pages in *Stress-Free Retirement* will set them all on the right course forever.

Now, I must point out that Fixed Indexed Annuities, and annuities in general, *do* charge fees; but it is a different type of fee structure than what is offered by most other financial vehicles. It is a fee structure much more controllable by the customer. Fees that can be avoided with proper planning and use of the FIA.

These particular fees, charged by most annuities, are called *surrender charges*. And a surrender charge works just like it sounds. It is a charge that is assessed on any amount withdrawn (surrendered) above the amount allowed by the *Penalty-Free Withdrawal* provision, a provision that most commonly allows

10 percent of the base annuity value per year to be withdrawn, beginning in the second year.

Please understand, and I can't stress this enough, *the scope of this book is not intended to fully educate you* on all the nuances of how each product, or aspect of each product, works. There are simply too many variances between products and states. For all of those details I highly encourage you to meet with a local professional who can answer all of your questions. Rather, the scope of this chapter, and of this entire book, is two things: one, to introduce you to the many benefits of the FIA, benefits you likely didn't know existed, and two, to equip you with enough knowledge that you can talk intelligently and ask the right questions when you do meet with your local representative.

But before we move on, let's take a high-altitude look at one example of how a *surrender charge* schedule might look within an FIA. Again, this is just a general example and not a specific reference to any particular product. See Figure 14.1.

Hypothetical Example of an FIA Surrender Charge Schedule

CONTRACT YEAR	PENALTY FREE WITHDRAWAL (PFW) ALLOWED	SURRENDER CHARGE FOR AMOUNTS WITHDRAWN ABOVE PFW
1	None	10%
2	10% of Base Annuity Value	9%
3	10% of Base Annuity Value	8%
4	10% of Base Annuity Value	7%
5	10% of Base Annuity Value	6%
6	10% of Base Annuity Value	5%
7	10% of Base Annuity Value	4%
8	10% of Base Annuity Value	3%
9	10% of Base Annuity Value	2%
10	10% of Base Annuity Value	1%
11+	Full Access to Entire Annuity Value	No More Surrender Charges

Figure 14.1

Now, I'd like to apply some actual numbers to the above schedule to see how this might play out in the real world. To do this, let's discuss an account owned by a hypothetical client named Lisa Smith.

Let's assume Mrs. Smith buys a $100,000 Fixed Indexed Annuity on January 1, 2013. During her first 12 months of ownership, January 2013 through December 2013, as you can see in Figure 14.1, Lisa is unable to withdraw any money out of her annuity without paying a 10-percent surrender charge on any amount she withdraws.

However, please note that Lisa *does* have liquidity. It's not like she can't get at her money in an emergency. She can. It's just that in order for her to do so within the first 12 months of the contract she would be charged a 10-percent surrender charge. And I must point out the obvious, because it won't be obvious to everyone – the surrender charge amount is assessed only on the amount removed from the annuity in that given year, *not* on the total account value.

So let's dig a little deeper in order to alleviate any concern that may linger regarding the surrender charge. Even the concern of withdrawing funds within the first year. To do this, let's look at another hypothetical example. Let's assume that Lisa *did* need to get at some of these funds within the first 12 months of the contract, and that she withdrew 10 percent of those funds, or $10,000. As stated in the surrender charge schedule in Figure 14.1, Lisa *would* be charged a 10-percent penalty on the entire $10,000 withdrawal, because during the first 12 months most FIAs do not offer a Penalty-Free Withdrawal feature. But, even if she did withdraw this in the first year, let's see how minor that really is in comparison with other possible options.

$10,000 x 10% fee = $1,000 paid in surrender charges

Figure 14.2

As you can see in Figure 14.2, the 10-percent surrender charge assessed to her withdrawal of $10,000 would cost Lisa $1,000. Right? But, let's look at it another way. Let's look at what that $1,000 charge represents as a percentage of Lisa's entire account value. See Figure 14.3.

$1,000 fee divided into $100,000 account value = 1%

$$\frac{\$1,000}{\$100,000} = .01 = 1\%$$

Figure 14.3

So what does a $1,000 fee represent to the total account value of Lisa's FIA? Just 1 percent – the *same amount* that some individuals pay *on an annual basis* on their currently managed money.

In other words, even if Lisa *did* need to get at a good portion of her money in the first year, when no Penalty-Free Withdrawal was allowed, it might still be no worse than most individuals pay *each and every year* currently. Does that make sense?

And the ramifications only get more significant from here, because in year two through year 10, in most cases, Lisa *is* able to get at 10 percent of her base annuity account value **each and every year without any penalty**. And again, if that's not enough liquidity, she can certainly take out more money, but she would be charged the corresponding surrender charge for any amount taken above the Penalty-Free Withdrawal.

So, let's look at another example. Let's say in year five Lisa faces a small financial emergency and needs to withdraw $20,000 from her annuity. For simplicity's sake, let's assume the Penalty-Free Withdrawal amount is based on the original purchase amount of $100,000. In other words, in this conservative example, $20,000 would equal a 20-percent withdrawal. Will Lisa be assessed a surrender charge? Yes. If you look at the graph in Figure 14.1 you see that based on this example, Lisa would be charged a 6-percent surrender charge on any amount she withdraws above $10,000. Since she withdrew $20,000 in this particular year, she would be charged 6 percent on the $10,000 above the PFW. So, in this example, Lisa would have to pay a total fee of $600 on that additional $10,000 she withdrew.

$10,000 X 6% = $600

Figure 14.4

But let's look at how minimal this amount really is in comparison with other common options in today's financial marketplace. If Lisa hadn't taken any other withdrawals up to this point that had exceeded the PFW amount, this would be the very first direct fee she would have been assessed during the entire five years the annuity had been in existence. Since her initial annuity purchase amount had been $100,000, that $600 charge translates into a total fee paid of only 0.6 percent of the entire account value. Think about that. The fee becomes an average of just 0.12 percent per year, if you average it out over the entire five-year time frame. And if that is the only time during the first 10 years that Lisa exceeds the PFW allowed, then during that 10-year period her average annual fee would be cut in half to just 0.06 percent per year. Do you know what that number is? *That represents six-one-hundredths of one percent.* Or .0006 if you want to see it in number form. In other words, next to nothing.

Here's yet another way to look at it. That $600 surrender charge that Lisa had to pay – just *one time,* the year in which she took out $10,000 above the PFW allowed – would result in total direct fees paid from her annuity, over a 10-year period, that were **95 percent less** than an account charging a 1-percent annual management fee, assuming a 5-percent annual growth on that account. See Figures

14.5 and 14.6 below for the year-by-year comparison of each.

Total Surrender Charges Paid by Lisa in Prior Example with FIA

YEAR	SURRENDER CHARGE EXPERIENCED BY LISA IN FIA
1	$0
2	$0
3	$0
4	$0
5	$600
6	$0
7	$0
8	$0
9	$0
10	$0
Total Fees Paid	**$600.00**

Figure 14.5

Total Fees Paid if Lisa Was Charged a 1-Percent Annual Fee Assuming 5-Percent Annual Growth

YEAR	ANNUAL ACCOUNT VALUE AT 5% GROWTH LESS 1% FEE	FEE BASED ON 1% ANNUAL CHARGE
1	$100,000.00	$1,000.00
2	$103,950.00	$1,039.50
3	$108,056.03	$1,080.56
4	$112,324.24	$1,123.24
5	$116,761.05	$1,167.61
6	$121,373.11	$1,213.73
7	$126,167.34	$1,261.67
8	$131,150.95	$1,311.51
9	$136,331.42	$1,363.31
10	$141,716.51	$1,417.17
Total Fees Paid Over 10 Years at 1%		$11,978.31

Figure 14.6

So, really, is the annuity's surrender charge a big deal? Not at all. As a matter of fact, Lisa could withdraw her entire annuity value in the first 12 months – all $100,000 – and the $10,000 she would pay in surrender charges would *still* be almost $2,000 *LESS* than she would pay for an account charging 1 percent per year over that same 10-year period. How's that for an eye opener?

And that does not take into account the fact that from year 11 on, many other options still charge 1 percent each and every year, while the FIA generally imposes no further surrender charge – ever. It's gone forever, making all funds totally accessible to the client without fear of any imposed fee.

Here's one last way to look at this comparison. If you understand that money within an FIA (or any annuity for that matter) is long-term money, and if you don't need to withdraw more than the PFW allows, then you will likely end up paying no surrender charges – ever. And according to my calculator, that's an infinite advantage over the $11,978.31 a typical account charging 1 percent per year would cost as shown in Figure 14.6.

So, there you have it. Was it a Pythagorian experience? Maybe not. But at least you no longer need to worry about walking off the edge of the earth the next time someone tells you the world is flat.

Chapter 15

The Breakup

So what now? That's always the question, isn't it? We acquire new knowledge, and soon we're faced with a choice – a fork in the road. Life calls us to make a decision.

In my second book, *The Retirement Miracle,* I have a quote page just before the preface, dedicated to a portion of Robert Frost's famous poem, *"The Road Not Taken."* I'm sure you know it, but it's so fitting to the question at hand that I want to quote it again.

"I shall be telling this with a sigh
Somewhere ages and ages hence:
Two roads diverged in a wood, and I –
I took the one less traveled by,
And that has made all the difference."

Doesn't that feel a bit like your situation right now? You've been walking your well-traveled path of volatility and risk for so long that it's all you know. It's comfortable. It's easy. It begs you to just "keep on keeping on." And up until today, that has been quite easy, because you didn't know another path even existed. But that's all changed. Now you do. And now you're facing the same decision as Robert Frost in his famous poem. *Do I venture onto this new and lightly traveled path, or do I forge ahead on the same money-losing path I've been on?*

Even though we don't know each other, I can feel your tension in that question. How? Through the lives of thousands who have come before you. Those who have stood at this same juncture and experienced the same fear of change. It's common. It's part of the human condition. Yet hundreds of thousands, maybe millions, have moved from fear to exhilaration as they embarked on this new journey. This new path.

If you could ask those who had chosen this new FIA path, prior to the spring of 2009, how they felt when the S&P® 500 had lost 52 percent of its value, yet their annuities hadn't lost a penny, what do you think they would say? Do you think they'd lament about not remaining in the market, exposed to all the craziness, wishing they could have watched their life's savings drop in half? Or do you think they'd be dancing a jig along this new path, marveling that they not only *didn't* lose a single penny, but that they also got to keep every previous gain that had ever been credited?

And while this new path provides many potential advantages, it is still not as common as you might think. There are hundreds of thousands who *have* chosen it, but there are hundreds of millions who have not. I want to give you two reasons why I believe this is true. And it has nothing to do with the viability of the strategy, but rather, as is usually the case, it is due to people's resistance to change.

The first reason I believe people don't choose this new path is because it requires action. Unfortunately, most people are averse to taking action – action of any kind – but especially when that action requires a change in the way things have always been done. The worst culprit being financial action. That's a real show-stopper. People delay financial change as long as humanly possible, and soon next week becomes next month, next month becomes next year, and next year becomes never. Their current and well-traveled path provides such a comfortable walk, such a familiar journey, that it's just easiest to stay right where they are, even if they are losing money.

The second reason I believe people don't choose this path may surprise you. It surprised me. Yet over the years, I have seen it with alarming regularity. It's the "nice-guy syndrome." When I define what that is, you may think, "Oh, that's *definitely* not me. I'd have no trouble with that." And I hope you wouldn't. But trust me, others do. Many others. It may even be the number-one reason why people *don't* embark on a new financial path. It is this. People hate, and I mean they detest, loathe, despise, and abhor, the idea of calling their existing financial representative and telling him they want to move their money somewhere else. It fills them with such dread that the phone instantly feels like a lead weight they are physically incapable of lifting.

As a matter of fact, I experienced this last week as I was having coffee with a good friend who is a successful entrepreneur. He was asking me about the content of the book he knew I was working on – this book – and as he listened to me explain it, he became intrigued. More than intrigued, actually. He said, "Wow. That sounds *exactly* like what I need to do. I'm done losing money. As a matter of fact, just a couple of months ago my retirement account finally got back to where it was 15 years ago."

I nodded with understanding, and before I could say a word, I watched the next thought cross his mind. A thought that caused his countenance to fall like a stone.

He said, "Wait. To take advantage of that product, I'd have to tell Dave I want to take my money somewhere else, wouldn't I?"

"Yep," I said.

"Oh man. That'd be brutal! It sounds like a great idea, and I *want* to do it. It's just that Dave's such a nice guy that I'd feel badly taking that money away from him. You know, he's done a pretty good job for me over the years, considering the circumstances. I'm really not sure if I could make that call."

I wanted to ask him, "If Dave has done such a good job over the years, then why is your account just *now* getting back to where it was 15 years ago?" But I refrained. (Yeah, you can call me Mr. Considerate.)

Maybe all of this sounds silly to you – all this blubber and worry about the financial representative's feelings – but my guess is that if you're currently working with someone, it probably makes perfect sense. Why would I guess this? Because it's incredibly common. More common than you would ever imagine.

One professional says it well. As we discussed this topic, here were his exact words.

"Patrick, I've personally met with hundreds of people who have been absolutely certain it was time for a change in regard to their financial representative. They knew it was time for the dreaded breakup – that it was time to call the existing representative or firm and let them know that they were going to be losing another customer.

"But in my experience, that soon-to-be ex-representative

makes life as difficult as humanly possible for the customer. He or she figuratively pitches a fit, promising new results if only the client will stay with him and give him one more chance to earn his business. And, the coup de grace is that he or she usually closes this conversation by pulling the ace of spades in the world of guilt – the *friendship* card. They say something like, 'Really, you're leaving me? You're leaving our friendship after all these years? After all I've done for you?' It's a ploy," he says. "Plain and simple. It has *nothing* to do with friendship but *everything* to do with commission."

The representative continues: "I always smile when I hear that a person's financial representative is a friend and that it will be too hard to 'break up' with him. It's at this point that I like to surprise these prospective clients by telling them very clearly that, if they are such good friends, then he really should not leave his current representative. I pause, momentarily, and then quickly continue by saying, 'I mean, why would you leave someone who is waiving all of your fees and commissions?' The answer is always the same, 'Of course he hasn't waived my fees,' the client says. And I reply, 'Oh, I just assumed that since you were such close friends, he was doing all his planning and work for free. But, what you're really telling me is that you pay the same rate as all of his other clients because you simply have a *professional business relationship* with someone who is a friend. Am I getting that right?' Almost always his or her head begins to nod up and down, slowly at first, but usually accelerating with each nod as the truth of that statement sinks in."

This representative told me he usually concludes with this statement: "If you've found a new product or strategy that meets your financial goals better than where you are now, then reward the individual who made you aware of it by bringing him your business. But also let him know that if he doesn't live up to your expectations, you'll be on your way with a handshake and all of your accounts in tow."

You see, I think it's critically important that you protect your family's finances as shrewdly as your current professional protects his own business, because that's exactly what they are, a business, at least in a financial sense. And just like any business, if you see a better path, you need to take it. I know feelings may get hurt, but really, in the end, are you more concerned about hurting your financial representative's feelings for a few days or your family's legacy for generations?

That's a simple choice in my mind.

PART 4: MORE THAN MONEY

Chapter 16

Share Your Stories

My grandfather on my mother's side was the youngest of nine. He was a tease. An adventurer. A tough and scrappy little guy. And more often than not he had his nose right in the middle of a heap of mischief, at least during most of his youth. But that's *exactly* what made his stories so marvelous.

He was born in 1913 in rural Arizona. Actually "rural" is an overstatement. His closest neighbor lived six miles away. There were seven kids in his entire school (not class, but school), and four of them were his brothers and sisters. And if there was one thing my grandfather could do, he could tell a great story.

When I was 12, he told me a story that I was convinced was the fish story to end all fish stories. We've all heard them, haven't we? The one that got away. The minnow that became a whale two hours after it was caught. And I was sure this story was just that – the ultimate fish yarn – as he told me about the giant halibut he caught in Alaska during his time in the Coast Guard … off the end of a dock … on a line wrapped around his hand.

Here's how it went.

"We were stationed in Alaska, and had just come into port. I wanted to go fishing, but I had two problems. One, I didn't have a boat. And two, I didn't have a pole. But I decided to go fishing anyway. I grabbed some line, a hook, and some bait, and I walked to the end of the dock our boat had just tied to and dropped a line in the water. And wouldn't you know, within about an hour, I had a monster halibut on the end of my line."

"No way!" I said, my 12-year-old skepticism on red-alert. "There's no way you caught a fish with your bare hands off the end of a dock."

"As a matter of fact, I did. And not just any fish, Patrick. A monster. A 163-pound halibut."

"Seriously? Are you making this up or did it really happen?"

"This is as real as the nose on your face," my grandpa said.

"How'd you get it in?" I asked.

"Well, after about four hours of slowly looping the line around and around my hand, I was starting to lose circulation, and my hand was cut to shreds, so I whistled at someone on the ship to get me a glove."

"No way!" I said again, my disbelief continuing to build. "You hauled up a 163-pound halibut with your bare hands?"

"Yep. Sure did. But boy that glove really helped."

I chuckled at the understatement. "Okay, so how'd you get it up on the dock?"

"Well, after the sailor who brought me the glove went back aboard the ship, he told the crew what I was doing. Soon I had an audience on the deck of the ship watching from above. They were cheering and yelling. Whooping and hollering. And when I finally got that big fish to the surface, they lowered the Coast Guard crane to haul that monster up onto the ship's deck. And you know the best part?"

"What?"

"It fed the entire Coast Guard ship that night – every single one of us – with fish to spare."

"Wow, Grandpa. That could be the greatest fish story I've ever heard. I wish I could have seen that guy."

"Well, as a matter of fact, I think you can," he said. "I believe I have a picture around here somewhere in one of these old photo albums."

And sure enough, he did. And any lingering skepticism immediately vanished as he dug out the album and showed me that magnificent, black and white picture of him standing on the end of that dock with a virtual whale hanging next to him by its tail.

Wow. What a story. But that wasn't his only one. He had dozens.

Like the time when he was 6, barefoot in the Arizona desert, tending the family's small flock of sheep. He came across a rattlesnake that he feared might hurt the animals in his care. And he did what every normal 6 year old would do. He took the shovel he was carrying and chopped that rattlesnake's head clean off. At 6! I could barely read a book or ride a bike at 6. And my grandpa was tending the family's prized flock and killing rattlesnakes with a shovel.

Or like the time when he stowed aboard a passing freight train from Seattle all the way to Los Angeles to see the 1932 Summer Olympics. It's a classic. During the day he'd climb on top of the boxcars and lay spread eagle, both to hold on and, also, so he wouldn't be seen. And then at night he'd climb down between two of the cars and loop his belt around one of the metal poles holding the cars together. He said it was the only way he could sleep without falling off during the night. Think about that. Today most of us complain about the lack of leg room in coach class; and here's my grandpa sleeping standing up, looped onto a moving freight train by a two-inch piece of worn leather. How crazy. How cool. And this is *my* bloodline.

Or like the time, or should I say *times*, when he and his brothers burned their family's house to the ground … two Fourth of Julys in a row. Yes, complete and total loss, two years in a row. Both times because he and his brothers threw firecrackers in the air that landed on their dry Arizona roof. How terrible. How amazing. And this is part of *my* history.

The stories continued, and I loved every one. I could sit for hours and just listen. And through the years I did exactly that. I so wish I'd recorded them, not only to hear those marvelous exploits again and again, but also to hear the joy in my grandpa's voice as he told them. I loved Hardenbrook family reunions, especially when my grandpa and all eight of his brothers and sisters were alive. There were hundreds of us in attendance, spanning four generations. We'd all gather around at the end of the first day and listen to new stories and old. One by one they'd pass the microphone, and we'd sit and watch the memories reengage after decades. Feeding off of each other. Reminiscing together.

I remember thinking. Wow. This is *my* lineage. *My* heritage. *My* family.

And now they're gone. All of them. None of the nine are still with us – but their stories are. The stories will live forever. Stories of moving and homesteading, of building careers and failed businesses, of raising kids and losing loved ones … and on and on and on. They were the stories of our family. The stories of our lives, both individual and corporate.

And now as I look back, I think *this* is wealth. *This* is how legacies are built and families are bonded. *This* is what life is really about. Inheriting money may be nice, but inheriting stories is sacred.

So why do I tell you this? Simple. Tell your stories. Tell them all. Tell your children. Tell your grandchildren. Tell them what life was like when you were their age. Tell them your greatest adventure as a teenager. Tell them how you met their grandmother or grandfather. Tell them your biggest failure. Your biggest regret. Tell them about the time you were most excited or about your greatest success. Tell them everything. They want to hear it. All of it. Trust me. If you make the time they'll want to listen. And they'll remember everything you tell them. And it will be these stories that will live on in your family's heritage for generations to come.

Remember, with all of the effort you put into planning, with all of your desire to leave a financial legacy when your time on earth is done, don't forget to give your family one of the most valuable gifts of all – your stories.

Chapter 17

Memories over Money

Decades ago, when my grandmother was still alive, I overheard her mention that she and her step-sister had finally reconciled after 50 years of total and complete estrangement. Fifty years! Can you believe that? Unfortunately, it happens all the time; yet many (maybe most) don't have a happy ending. Fortunately, for my grandmother, hers did. She and her step-sister entered eternity as the best of friends. Unfortunately, neither of them could do anything to make up for all of those lost years. Years that would have added meaning and texture to both of their lives.

And you'll never guess what started this half-century dispute. A set of china. (Yes, as in dishes.) It's a long story, as it usually is. But the short answer is that this dispute originated with "STUFF." While that seems totally ridiculous to me, I fear it's far too common.

I remember playing golf a few years ago with a couple of guys I didn't know. As we hacked around the course together, one of them shared with me his perspective on "stuff." He said, "I don't care that much about stuff. The way I see it, the only things we can take with us when we die are our memories and our relationships."

Wow. Good words. As a matter of fact, I think memories and relationships just may be the currency of eternity.

But if that really is the case, then why do most people spend their lives acting like it's all of their "stuff" that matters most? Their money. Their things. The last time I checked, "stuff" *always* gets left behind. As the old adage goes, "You never see a hearse pulling a U-Haul."

So, if we can't bring it with us, what *should* we do with it? How should we use our money and our things? Those are deeply important questions. Questions we often contemplate too late in life, just as the twilight is fading to darkness.

However, I want to help you think through this right now, while you still have all of your options. And I'm going to propose to you that the highest calling for your stuff, its greatest purpose, is to use it to build those two precious things that *do* last forever – memories and relationships.

How can you do this? I think you inherently know; but, just in case, I'll make it absolutely clear. Spend it. Not wastefully or frivolously. Not in a way that puts your living expenses in jeopardy. But, rather, spend it in a way that maximizes all of that extra money, all of the "stuff" that is going to get left behind, in such a way as to bless those you love and build special memories that you will all carry into eternity. Isn't that what we really want? To be remembered with fondness. To know we made a difference in the lives of others and left our mark.

For example, instead of stockpiling that extra $15,000 or $20,000 in some sterile and impersonal bank account, take your children and grandchildren – your entire gaggle of offspring – on a cruise. Let them experience a part of the world they would never otherwise see. Enjoy dining together each night with a view of the vast Pacific. Explore ancient cultures as you hold your 8-year-old granddaughter's hand. Show them what a "cool" 70-year-old grandmother looks like as you zip-line through the treetops of Costa Rica. Or fish the majestic rivers of Canada. Think about all the things you could do. Take them to see Mickey Mouse. Or a sunrise in the Greek Isles. Or the Northern Lights in Alaska. Think about all of those incredible memories. Isn't that infinitely more valuable than leaving them money? Doesn't that make your heart sing just a little louder?

And it can be even more significant than that. Your "stuff" can create blessings far beyond just your own family. Think what a blessing your money could be for those who are literally thirsting and starving to death around the world. For those whose lives are being devastated by natural disasters and human atrocities. Individuals you may never know but can certainly bless.

Doesn't that get your blood pumping just a little faster? To know that you used whatever you had, whether it was a little or a lot, to be a blessing to others? I can't think of a higher calling for our finances or many greater joys.

And think about this. If we consider individuals wise who invest their money for 30 or 40 years, how much more wisdom would we assign to individuals who invest for eternity? Who build a storehouse of memories and relationships that will last forever? Who gives to those who would otherwise perish? Now that's the kind of investment I want to make.

And think how amusing it would be if, as you're crossing the finish line of life, you had planned so well and spent so lavishly on others, that the last check you wrote, the one to the undertaker, actually bounced. Ha. How fun would that be? I'll bet your kids would double over with laughter knowing that you invested everything into building memories with them and their children. Who knows? Maybe they'd even be willing to write the check to get you buried.

Okay, while that last thought is clearly an exaggeration for the sake of humor, I'm sure you get the picture. Don't stress about spending the money you've saved. That's exactly what it's for. Give it. Spend it. And use it to make a difference in the lives of others and to create a life full of blessed memories and relationships. If you do, I can most certainly guarantee you one thing – a life well lived.

Epilogue

Now what? That's *really* the question. Isn't it? What are you going to do with this new information? Do you like the idea of putting your money on autopilot? Of escaping the ravages of stock market volatility? Of freeing yourself up to live a life of significance as described in chapters 17 and 18? Does the idea of protecting your retirement nest egg from loss instill a sense of peace and tranquility? I hope so. It should.

It is my desire that this book has given you a deep sense of hope for your future, not only hope for your financial future, but also hope for the significant legacy you can leave behind with the generations that will follow.

But back to the questions you need to answer today. *Now what? What's my next step?*

I'm sure there are many possible answers to those questions. Many roads that can lead to success and prosperity. But I am also equally certain that there is one road that will lead to financial mediocrity as well. And that is the choice of the status quo – to do nothing. To ignore. To procrastinate.

Only you will know what's right for you. But only after you've compared your options. So that's what I encourage you to do today. Compare. Take a look. See what this new path has to offer. And the best way to do that, as I've mentioned many times throughout this book, is to meet with a local, knowledgeable, and licensed representative. One who can steer you in the right direction with *your* needs and *your* desires as priority number one.

As I end this book I want to say thank you for spending a little time with me. I hope these pages have been helpful in some way; and I wish you all the best in your future endeavors as well as a prosperous and *Stress-Free Retirement*.

Endnotes

"Standard & Poor's," "S&P 500," "Standard & Poor's 500," and "500" are all registered trademarks of The McGraw-Hill Companies, Inc. These products are not sponsored, endorsed, sold or promoted by Standard & Poor's and Standard & Poor's make no representation regarding the advisability of purchasing these products.

[i] https://www.google.com/advisor/uscd?bsp&s=1&kw=CD%20rates&group=GenericRadio&q=cd+rates (In a search of "best performing cds" on 12/1/2011, this was the top paid advertised listing.)

[ii] http://en.wikipedia.org/wiki/Fractional_reserve_banking#Example_of_deposit_multiplication

[iii] http://www.taxadmin.org/fta/rate/ind_inc.pdf

iv   http://www.usinflationcalculator.com/inflation/current-inflation-rates/

v   MoneyChimp.com: http://www.moneychimp.com/features/market_cagr.htm (Based on year-end data through 2011.)

vi   MoneyChimp.com: http://www.moneychimp.com/features/market_cagr.htm (Based on year-end data through 2011.)

vii   Much of this chapter was taken from Chapter 6 of my book *The Retirement Miracle*. That chapter has made such a significant difference in the way individuals understand investment returns that it needed to be updated and included in this book.

viii   Much of this chapter was taken from Chapter 12 of my book *The Retirement Miracle*.

About the Author

Patrick Kelly is the author of *Tax-Free Retirement* (2007) and *The Retirement Miracle* (2011), which have together sold more than 1 million copies. Patrick has spent much of the last six years on a national platform delivering his unique message to over 100,000 financial professionals from coast to coast and has become one of the industry's most sought-after speakers. Patrick's strong counsel for everyone within the financial industry to practice a "client first" philosophy is the centerpiece of all his messages. One of his greatest passions is to help consumers understand they are able to step off the roller coaster of fear and loss and onto the peace-filled road of growth and stability.

Patrick lives in the Puget Sound area with his wife and their four children.